Go Programming for Microservices

Build Scalable, High-Performance Applications with Ease

Tommy Clark

1

Discover other Books in the Series

"Go Programming for Beginners: Master Go from Scratch with Easy-to-Follow Steps"

"Web Applications with Go: Unlock the Power of Go for Real-World Web Server Development"

"System Programming with Go: Unlock the Power of System Calls, Networking, and Security with Practical Golang Projects"

"Go Programming for Backend: The Developer's Blueprint for Efficiency and Performance"

"Web Security with Go: Build Safe and Resilient Applications"

"Network Automation with Go: Automate Network Operations and Build Scalable Applications with Go"

"Effective Debugging in Go: Master the Skills Every Go Developer"

Disclaimer

The information provided **"Go Programming for Microservices: Build Scalable, High-Performance Applications with Ease"** by Tommy Clark is intended solely for educational and informational purposes. While every effort has been made to ensure the accuracy and completeness of the content, the author and publisher make no guarantees regarding the results that may be achieved by following the instructions or techniques described in this book.

This book is not a substitute for professional advice, consultation, or training. Readers are encouraged to seek appropriate professional guidance for specific issues or challenges they may encounter, particularly in commercial or critical environments.

The author and publisher disclaim all liability for any loss, damage, or inconvenience arising directly or indirectly from the use or misuse of the information contained within this book. Any reliance on the information provided is at the reader's own risk.

Introduction

High-performance, scalable apps are more important than ever in the ever changing digital world of today. The architecture of these apps is essential to accomplishing the objectives of organizations, which include improving user experiences, optimizing operations, and growing their services. Presenting microservices, an architectural paradigm that provides quick deployment, robustness, and adaptability. The Go programming language, a strong, effective tool that is ideal for creating reliable microservices, enters the picture here.

Welcome to **"Go Programming for Microservices: Build Scalable, High-Performance Applications with Ease."** The purpose of this book is to walk you through the fundamentals of microservices architecture and equip you with the knowledge and abilities needed to use Go to create high-performance apps. Whether you're a seasoned developer trying to add more tools to your toolbox or a novice excited to learn about microservices, this thorough guide offers insightful analysis and useful examples to improve your knowledge and skills.

Why Travel?

Go, sometimes referred to as Golang, is praised for its effectiveness and simplicity. Google developed it to overcome the drawbacks of previous programming languages, especially when it came to large-scale distributed systems. Go is a great option for developing microservices because of its many capabilities, which include effective memory management, built-in concurrency support, and a robust standard library. Writing clear, maintainable code that performs exceptionally well is possible with Go.

Things You'll Discover

As you read this book, you will learn:

Microservices Foundations: Recognize the fundamentals of microservices architecture, especially its advantages over conventional monolithic designs. Go Language Fundamentals: Learn about Go's main characteristics, including as its data types, syntax, and concurrency model, all of which are crucial for creating microservices.

Building Microservices: Detailed instructions for creating, putting into practice, and deploying microservices with Go, along with recommended practices to guarantee their smooth interoperability.

Monitoring and Testing: Discover efficient methods for testing your
microservices and keeping an eye on how well they operate in real-world settings.

Real-World Instances: Learn from real-world examples that demonstrate the application of Go and microservices ideas.

Who Should Read This Book?

Whether you are a seasoned software engineer, a team

leader, or someone looking to transition into the world of microservices, this book will equip you with the knowledge to effectively leverage the Go programming language. It is catered to individuals keen on understanding how Go can help build efficient, scalable applications that can adapt to changing user demands.

Join the Journey

As you embark on this journey into Go programming for microservices, prepare to challenge yourself, expand your knowledge, and enhance your skills. By the end of this book, you will not only comprehend the principles of microservices but also be capable of designing and implementing your own high- performance applications with Go.

Let's dive in and start building scalable, high-performance applications with ease!

Chapter 1: Introduction to Microservices and Go

The rise of cloud computing and the increasing demand for complex, distributed applications have given birth to microservices—a software architectural style that structures an application as a collection of loosely coupled services. This chapter explores the concept of microservices, their benefits and challenges, and how the Go programming language aligns perfectly with this paradigm.

Understanding Microservices

Microservices architecture is a design approach that breaks applications into smaller, independent services that can be developed, deployed, and scaled individually. Each service is built around a specific business capability and communicates with others over a network, typically using RESTful APIs or message brokers. This architectural style contrasts with the traditional monolithic approach, where an entire application is tightly integrated and often becomes cumbersome to manage as it grows.

Key Characteristics of Microservices

Modularity: Each microservice encapsulates a specific business function, allowing developers to work on different services independently. This modularity promotes clearer design and easier maintenance.

Scalability: Microservices can be scaled independently

based on demand. If a particular service requires more resources, it can be scaled without impacting the entire application.

Technology Agnostic: Different microservices can be written in different programming languages and can leverage various databases and frameworks. This polyglot nature allows teams to choose the best tools for the specific problem at hand.

Resilience: With microservices, the failure of one service does not necessarily lead to the failure of the entire application. This isolation can improve the overall reliability and stability of the system.

Continuous Delivery: The modular nature of microservices supports continuous delivery and deployment practices. Teams can deploy updates to individual services without waiting for the entire application to be redeployed.

Challenges of Microservices

While the microservices approach offers numerous benefits, it is not without challenges:

Complexity: Managing multiple services introduces complexity in terms of deployment, monitoring, and communication between services. Orchestrating these services requires careful planning and sophisticated deployment strategies.

Data Management: With decentralized data

management, ensuring data consistency across services can be difficult. Each microservice often manages its own database, complicating transactions that span multiple services.

Network Latency: Communication between services over the network can introduce latency. It's crucial to optimize service interactions and understand the implications of network calls on performance.

Testing and Debugging: Testing microservices can be more complex than testing monolithic applications. Ensuring that all services interact correctly adds another layer of difficulty in both development and production environments.

The Go Programming Language

Go, also known as Golang, is a statically typed, compiled language designed by Google that has gained popularity for its simplicity, performance, and strong concurrency features. These characteristics make Go an excellent choice for building microservices.

Why Choose Go for Microservices?

Performance: Go's compiled nature allows for high-performance applications. The language's efficiency makes it suitable for building services that require fast execution and low latency.

Concurrency: Go's goroutines make it easy to handle multiple tasks simultaneously, providing an elegant solution to concurrency that is essential for microservices architecture.

Simplicity: Go's syntax is clear and straightforward, which helps reduce the learning curve for teams and enables faster development cycles.

Strong Standard Library: Go offers an extensive standard library, especially for building web servers, handling HTTP requests, and performing JSON manipulation, which are crucial for developing microservices.

Ease of Deployment: Go binaries are statically linked, making deployment straightforward. Developers can easily compile a single binary that contains everything needed to run a service, ensuring a consistent and reliable deployment process.

And So, The Journey Begins

As we dive deeper into the world of microservices and Go in this book, we will explore various patterns, practices, and tools that complement the microservices architecture. Through hands-on examples, best practices, and architectural principles, this book will provide you with the knowledge and skills necessary to design, develop, and deploy microservices in Go effectively.

Throughout our journey, we will be challenged to think critically about the systems we build and the trade-offs involved. With the right understanding, tools, and techniques, microservices can empower developers and organizations to create robust, scalable, and maintainable applications.

Understanding Microservices Architecture

This chapter delves into the core concepts of microservices architecture, its advantages, challenges, and best practices for implementation. By understanding microservices, developers and organizations can better navigate the complexities of modern software development and delivery.

What Are Microservices?

Microservices architecture is an approach to software development where a large application is composed of small, independently deployable services. Each service is focused on a specific business capability and communicates with other services through well-defined APIs. This contrasts with monolithic architecture, where all components of an application are tightly coupled and interdependent.

Characteristics of Microservices

Independent Deployment: Each microservice can be developed, deployed, and scaled independently. This autonomy allows teams to iterate quickly and deploy updates without affecting other services.

Single Responsibility: Microservices are designed around a specific business function, adhering to the principle of single responsibility. This makes them easier to manage and reason about.

Decentralized Data Management: Unlike monolithic systems that usually rely on a single database, microservices often have their own databases tailored to their specific needs, enhancing adaptability and reducing the risk of data corruption.

Technology Agnostic: Services can be built using different programming languages and technologies, allowing teams to choose the best tools for each specific job without being constrained by a common technology stack.

Resilience: The failure of one microservice does not necessarily bring down the entire application. This isolation improves the overall resilience of the system.

Advantages of Microservices Architecture

Scalability: Microservices can be scaled individually based on demand. For example, if a specific service experiences high traffic, only that service can be scaled up, optimizing resource usage.

Faster Time to Market: Agile teams can develop and deploy services rapidly, resulting in quicker releases and a more responsive approach to changing business requirements.

Improved Fault Isolation: If one microservice fails, it does not affect the entirety of the application. This allows for better error handling and recovery strategies.

Enhanced Collaboration: Independent microservices enable cross-functional teams to work on different services simultaneously, fostering collaboration and faster decision-making.

Better Resource Utilization: Microservices can be optimized for specific services, allowing for more efficient use of computing resources and costs.

Challenges of Microservices Architecture

Despite its many advantages, adopting microservices architecture also poses challenges:

Complexity: The system as a whole becomes more complex as the number of services increases. Managing inter-service communication, data consistency, and security becomes critical.

Service Coordination: Orchestrating the various microservices can be challenging, requiring robust application programming interfaces (APIs) and possibly service mesh technology.

Data Management: With decentralized data storage, ensuring consistency and managing transactions across services can become complex.

Latency: Network calls between services can introduce latency. Optimizing communication patterns is essential to mitigate performance issues.

DevOps Expertise: Organizations need to invest in DevOps capabilities to manage the continuousdeployment and integration of multiple services.

Best Practices for Implementing Microservices

To harness the benefits of microservices while minimizing the challenges, consider the following bestpractices:

Define Services Properly: Carefully analyze business requirements to define service boundaries. A well-defined service should encapsulate a specific business capability.

Leverage API Gateways: Use API gateways to manage and route requests to the appropriate services. This can simplify client interactions and provide a layer of security.

Integrate Monitoring and Logging: Implement centralized logging and monitoring solutions to track the health and performance of each microservice. This is crucial for troubleshooting and understanding system behavior.

Implement Fault Tolerance: Design services with fault tolerance in mind. Techniques like circuit breakers and retries can help maintain system reliability.

Automate Testing and Deployment: Adopt automated testing and continuous integration/continuousdeployment (CI/CD) practices to streamline development and reduce the risk of introducing errors.

Manage Data Consistency: Use eventual consistency

models and patterns like the Saga pattern to manage distributed transactions and maintain data integrity.

By understanding the fundamentals of microservices, their advantages and challenges, and adhering to best practices, teams can successfully navigate the complexities of software development in a microservices environment. As organizations strive for digital transformation, embracing microservices may well be a significant step toward achieving their goals in scalability, maintainability, and overall efficiency.

The Power of Go for Microservices Development

With its promise of splitting complex applications into manageable, independently deployable units, microservices architecture has transformed how developers think about application design. Among the many programming languages that support this architectural style, Go, often referred to as Golang, stands out for its simplicity, performance, and concurrency capabilities. This chapter delves into the benefits of using Go for microservices development, exploring its features, ecosystem, and how it enhances productivity and efficiency in modern application development.

Understanding Microservices Architecture

Before we dive into the specifics of Go, it's crucial to understand the principles of microservices architecture. Microservices represent an architectural style that structures an application as a collection of loosely coupled services. Each service is designed to execute a specific business function and can be developed, deployed, and maintained independently. This approach offers several advantages, including:

Scalability: Services can be scaled independently based on demand.
Resilience: Failure of one service does not impact the overall system.
Flexibility: Teams can use different technologies and frameworks for different services.
Faster Time to Market: Smaller, independent teams can iterate quickly on their respective services.

Given these benefits, the choice of programming language for developing microservices becomes paramount, as it directly affects developer productivity, system performance, and overall application maintainability.

Go: An Overview

Go, designed by Google engineers Robert Griesemer, Rob Pike, and Ken Thompson, was released to the public in 2009. The language has grown rapidly in popularity within the developer community, thanks to its strengths in performance, simplicity, and effective concurrency management. Here are some of the core features that make Go a compelling choice for microservices development:

Simplicity: Go's syntax is clean and straightforward, making it easy to read and write. This simplicity helps reduce the cognitive load on developers, allowing them to focus on building functionalities rather than wrestling with complex language constructs.

Efficient Concurrency: Go has built-in support for concurrent programming through goroutines and channels. This makes it easier to handle multiple tasks simultaneously which is essential in microservices where numerous services often need to interact with each other performantly.

Performance: Go is a compiled language, which means it translates code directly into machine code. This allows Go applications to run at impressive speeds, often comparable to those written in C or C++. Performance is critical in microservices, particularly where latency is a concern.

Strong Standard Library: Go comes with a rich standard library that provides a wide range of built-in functions for handling tasks such as web services, networking, and encryption. This extensive library allows developers to build robust services without relying heavily on external packages.

Cross-Platform Capability: Go supports cross-compilation, enabling developers to build applications for different platforms and architectures easily. This feature is invaluable in microservices environments where services might run on a variety of systems.

Static Typing and Efficiency: The static type system in Go catches many errors at compile time, which can speed up the development process. Tools like `go vet` and static analysis libraries can help developers enforce best practices and identify issues early in the development lifecycle.

Advantages of Using Go for Microservices

Incorporating Go into microservices development presents numerous advantages: ### 1. Rapid Development
Due to Go's simplicity and verbose documentation, teams can significantly shorten their development cycles. Go's conventions, such as idiomatic error handling, lead to clearer code, which simplifies maintenance. This rapid iteration makes Go particularly attractive in a microservices context where services need constant updates.

2. Robustness and Maintainability

The simplicity and clarity of Go's syntax promote robust and maintainable code. Developers can quickly onboard new team members without steep learning curves, providing an advantage in team scalability and distribution. The simplicity of Go also allows writing clean interfaces for services, enhancing the overall architecture.

3. Excellent Tooling

Go is equipped with a rich ecosystem of tools that support the entire development lifecycle, from code formatting with `gofmt` to dependency management with `go modules`. Tools like `go test`, `go doc`, and others streamline the processes of testing, documentation, and package management, facilitating a smoother development workflow for microservices.

4. Scalability

Go's lightweight goroutines make it highly scalable. When building microservices, handling many requests concurrently is paramount. Goroutines utilize less memory than traditional threads, allowing microservices to handle thousands of concurrent operations without significant overhead.

5. Deployment and Docker Compatibility

Go's statically linked binaries eliminate the need for dependencies at runtime, which makes deployment straightforward. This feature aligns perfectly with the containerization trend within microservices, particularly using Docker. With Docker, developers can encapsulate Go applications along with their runtime environment, ensuring consistency across development, testing, and production.

Case Studies: Go in Action

Several high-profile tech companies have embraced Go for microservices development, showcasing its strengths in real-world applications:

Google: Not surprisingly, Google uses Go for numerous internal services due to its performance and concurrency capabilities. The programming language was designed with large-scale distributed systems in mind, making it a perfect fit for Google's architecture.

Uber: Uber adopted Go for developing parts of their microservices ecosystem due to its speed and efficiency. The company required a programming language that could handle a high volume of requests andtransactions, which Go accomplished remarkably.

Dropbox: To improve performance and reduce latency, Dropbox transitioned some services to Go.They found that Go's efficiency boosted their service response times considerably.

Chapter 2: Setting Up Your Development Environment

Setting up your development environment is a crucial step in the process of learning and developing any programming language. For Go—a language designed for simplicity and efficiency—having the right tools and configurations can streamline your workflow and enhance productivity. In this chapter, we will guide you through the steps to set up a robust development environment for Go, covering installation, editor configuration, version management, and much more.

2.1 Installing Go

The first step in setting up your Go development environment is to install the Go programming language itself. The latest version of Go can be downloaded from the official website, [golang.org](https://golang.org/dl/).

2.1.1 Downloading Go

Visit the Download Page: Go to the official downloads page of Go.
Choose Your Operating System: Select the appropriate installer for your operating system (Windows, macOS, or Linux).
Download the Installer: Click the download link, and save the installer on your machine. ### 2.1.2 Installing Go
Windows: Run the downloaded `.msi` installer and follow the prompts. The installer will typically place Go in `C:\Go`.

macOS: Open the downloaded `.pkg` file and follow the installation instructions.
Linux: You can install Go by extracting the archive. Open a terminal and run the followingcommands:

```bash
wget https://golang.org/dl/go1.x.linux-amd64.tar.gz sudo tar -C /usr/local -xzf go1.x.linux-amd64.tar.gz
```

After installation, you will need to add Go's binary directory to your PATH. This can be done by adding thefollowing line to your shell profile file (`.bashrc`, `.bash_profile`, `.zshrc`, etc.):

```bash
export PATH=$PATH:/usr/local/go/bin
```

After making changes, make sure to reload your shell or source the profile file using `source ~/.bashrc`.### 2.1.3 Verifying the Installation
To verify that Go was installed correctly, open a terminal or command prompt and type:

```bash
go version
```

```
```

You should see the Go version displayed, indicating that the installation was successful. ## 2.2 Setting Up Your Workspace
Go uses a workspace structure that allows you to manage your projects efficiently. The workspace is typically defined by a directory where your Go code resides.

2.2.1 Creating Your Go Workspace

Create a Directory: Open your terminal and create a directory for your Go projects. For instance, let's name it `go-workspace`.

```bash
mkdir $HOME/go-workspace
```

Setting Environment Variables: The Go ecosystem relies heavily on certain environment variables. Set the `GOPATH` to your workspace directory by adding the following line to your profile file:

```bash
export GOPATH=$HOME/go-workspace
```

Also, ensure that your PATH includes the `bin` directory of your workspace:

```bash
export PATH=$PATH:$GOPATH/bin
```

```
```

Confirm the Setup: Restart your terminal or source your profile file, then run:

```bash
echo $GOPATH
```

You should see the path to your Go workspace. ## 2.3 Choosing an Editor or IDE
A good code editor or integrated development environment (IDE) can significantly enhance your productivity. There are several options available that support Go development.

2.3.1 Popular Editors and IDEs

Visual Studio Code: A widely-used, customizable editor with excellent Go support through extensions such as `Go` by the Go team.
GoLand: A paid IDE by JetBrains that offers advanced features specifically tailored for Go development.
Vim/Neovim: Minimalistic editors that have plugins available for Go support, such as `vim-go`.
Sublime Text: Another popular text editor that can be configured for Go development with suitable packages.

2.3.2 Configuring VS Code for Go

If you choose Visual Studio Code, here's how to set it up for Go:

Install VS Code: Download and install Visual Studio

Code from the [official website](https://code.visualstudio.com/).
Install the Go Extension:
Launch VS Code.
Navigate to the extensions view by clicking on the Extensions icon in the Activity Bar.
Search for "Go" and install the official extension provided by the Go team.
Set up Go Tools: When you open a Go file for the first time, the Go extension may prompt you to install necessary Go tools. Follow the prompts to ensure you have all the essentials.

2.4 Managing Go Versions

As you delve deeper into Go, you may need to work with multiple versions of the language. To achieve this, managing your Go versions with a tool like `gvm` (Go Version Manager) can be beneficial.

2.4.1 Installing GVM

To install GVM, follow these steps:

Open your terminal and run:

```bash
bash <(curl -s https://raw.githubusercontent.com/moovweb/gvm/master/binscripts/gvm-installer)
```

Follow the instructions provided by the installer.

After installation, you may need to set up your shell profile to include GVM:

```bash
source ~/.gvm/scripts/gvm
```

2.4.2 Using GVM

To install a specific version of Go with GVM:

```bash
gvm install go1.x.x
```

You can switch between installed versions using:

```bash
gvm use go1.x.x
```

By this point, you should have a fully working Go development environment. You've installed the Go language, configured your workspace, chosen an editor, and set up version management. With these essentials in place, you're ready to embark on your journey into Go programming, confident that your tools will support your development needs. In the next chapter, we'll begin exploring the foundational concepts of the Go language.

Installing and Configuring Go

Developed by Google, it was first released in 2009 and has

since gained immense popularity, especially for building web servers, microservices, and cloud-based applications. Its built-in support for concurrent programming, garbage collection, and a rich standard library make it an excellent choice for modern software development.

Before diving into Go's features and capabilities, one must first get it installed and properly configured. This chapter will guide you through the steps needed to install Go on various operating systems, set up your development environment, and ensure the configuration works smoothly.

System Requirements

To ensure a successful installation, ensure your machine meets the following minimum requirements:

Operating System: Windows, macOS, or a modern Linux distribution.
Processor: 64-bit architecture is recommended.
Disk Space: At least 200 MB of free disk space. ## Step 1: Downloading Go
The first step in installing Go is to download it from the official website.

Visit the Go Website: Navigate to [golang.org](https://golang.org/dl/). You will see a list of downloadable binaries for different operating systems.
Choose Your Version: Select the appropriate binary for your operating system. For most users, the latest stable version is recommended.

Step 2: Installing Go ### On Windows

Execute the Installer: Double-click the downloaded `.msi` file. This will launch the Go installation wizard.

Follow the Instructions: Click through the installation steps. You can either accept the default installation path (C:\Go) or choose a custom directory.

Set Environment Variables: The installer typically sets the necessary environment variables automatically. If you need to configure them manually:

Open **Control Panel** > **System and Security** > **System** > **Advanced system settings**.

Click on the **Environment Variables** button.

Under **System Variables**, add a new variable `GOPATH` pointing to your workspace directory (default is `C:\Users\<YourUsername>\go`).

On macOS

Use Homebrew (Recommended): Open your Terminal and run the following command:
```bash
brew install go
```

Manual Installation:
Unpack the downloaded `.tar.gz` file into the `/usr/local` directory.

Open Terminal and run the following command:
```bash
sudo tar -C /usr/local -xzf go$VERSION.darwin-amd64.tar.gz
```

Replace `$VERSION` with the version number you

downloaded.

Set your PATH: Add Go binary to your PATH by adding the following line to your `~/.bash_profile` or `~/.zshrc`:
```bash
export PATH=$PATH:/usr/local/go/bin
```

Then, run `source ~/.bash_profile` or `source ~/.zshrc`.

On Linux

Use a Package Manager: For Ubuntu and Debian-based distributions, Open your terminal and run:
```bash
sudo apt update
sudo apt install golang-go
```

Manual Installation:
Download the `.tar.gz` file for Linux from the Go website. Extract it to `/usr/local` using:
```bash
sudo tar -C /usr/local -xzf go$VERSION.linux-amd64.tar.gz
```

Set your PATH: Similarly to macOS, add Go binary to your PATH by editing your `~/.bashrc` or `~/.profile`:
```bash
export PATH=$PATH:/usr/local/go/bin
```

Then apply the changes with:
```bash
source ~/.bashrc
```

Step 3: Verifying the Installation

After the installation, it's essential to verify your setup:

Open a terminal or command prompt.
Type the following command:
```bash
go version
```

If Go is installed correctly, it will display the installed version, confirming that the installation was successful.

Step 4: Setting Up Your Workspace

Go is designed with a specific workspace structure. By default, your workspace consists of the following directories:

** `src`:** Source files are stored here.
** `pkg`:** Compiled package objects.
** `bin`:** Compiled executable files. To set up your workspace:
Create a directory for your Go workspace:
```bash
mkdir -p $GOPATH/src
```

Add your workspace directory to your PATH by modifying your shell configuration file (like `.bashrc`, `.bash_profile`, or `.zshrc`), adding:
```bash
export GOPATH=$HOME/go
export PATH=$PATH:$GOPATH/bin
```

```
```

After making changes, ensure to `source` your configuration file to apply the modifications. ## Step 5: Writing Your First Go Program

Now that you've installed and configured Go, it's time to write your first program:

Create a new directory within your `src` folder for your project:
```bash
mkdir -p $GOPATH/src/hellocd $GOPATH/src/hello
```

Create a new file named `main.go`:
```go
package mainimport "fmt"
func main() { fmt.Println("Hello, World!")
}
```

Compile and run your first Go application:
```bash
go run main.go
```

You should see `Hello, World!` printed in the terminal, confirming that your Go setup is working correctly.

With Go installed and configured, you're now ready to explore its rich features and capabilities. This chapter provided you with a step-by-step guide on how to install Go on different operating systems, set up your workspace, and run your first Go program. Through practice and exploration, you will undoubtedly unlock the power of Go and enhance your development workflow. In upcoming chapters, we will delve deeper into Go's syntax, paradigms, and libraries, opening the door to writing robust applications in Go.

Tools and Frameworks for Go Microservices

Go (or Golang), a statically typed, compiled programming language created at Google, is especially well- suited for microservices because of its lightweight nature, concurrency support, and simplicity. This chapter explores various tools and frameworks that facilitate the development of Go microservices, enhancing productivity, maintainability, and scalability.

1. The Go Language: A Brief Overview

Go is designed to be simple and efficient, with built-in support for concurrent programming through goroutines and channels. Its powerful standard library, combined with a robust ecosystem of third-party packages, makes it an excellent choice for building microservices. Some features that make Go particularly attractive for microservices development include:

Concurrency: Go's goroutines and channels make it easy to handle multiple tasks simultaneously.
Performance: With speed comparable to that of languages like C++, Go is great for high-performance applications.

Simplicity: The language syntax is straightforward, minimizing the learning curve for new developers.
Strong Typing: Go's type system provides safety and clarity when working on complex systems. ## 2. Go Microservices Frameworks
When building microservices, leveraging frameworks can speed up development and abstract away many of the complexities involved. Below are some popular frameworks for developing microservices in Go.

2.1. Gin

Gin is a lightweight web framework that is high in performance and productivity. Its focus on speed makes it a great choice for building RESTful APIs for microservices.

Key Features:
HTTP middleware support
JSON serialization
User-friendly routing
Error management
Built-in validation### 2.2. Echo
Echo is another high-performance, extensible, minimalist web framework for Go. It features a fast HTTProuter and provides robust middleware support.

Key Features:
Middleware support for logging, CORS, and authentication
Template rendering
Built-in data binding and validation
HTTP/2 support### 2.3. Revel

Revel is a high-productivity web framework that promotes

convention over configuration. It offers a lot out of the box, including a built-in web server, and is suitable for larger applications.

Key Features:
Hot reloading for development
Built-in testing framework
Comprehensive routing system
Modular design with plugins

3. Service Discovery and API Gateway

As microservices architecture grows, the need for efficient communication between services becomes critical. Service discovery and API gateways serve as central points of control.

3.1. Consul

Consul is a tool for service discovery that provides a distributed key-value store for configuration and service registration. It allows microservices to find each other easily and manage their health checks.

Key Features:
Health monitoring
Multi-datacenter support
Key-value storage
Service mesh capabilities ### 3.2. Istio
Istio is an open-source service mesh that provides a way to manage microservices. It offers advanced traffic management, security features, and observability without requiring changes to application code.

Key Features:
Traffic routing and load balancing
Security and policy enforcement
Distributed tracing
API management capabilities### 3.3. Traefik
Traefik is a modern HTTP reverse proxy and load balancer that makes dealing with microservices easier. It can automatically discover services and route traffic based on various rules.

Key Features:
Dynamic configuration
Middleware support
CORS configuration
Let's Encrypt integration for SSL management## 4. Data Management
Microservices often need to interact with databases or other data storage solutions. Choosing the right database technology and an ORM (Object-Relational Mapping) library can simplify data management.

4.1. GORM

GORM is a popular ORM library for Golang, which allows developers to interact with databases using Go structures. It supports multiple database backends, including PostgreSQL, MySQL, and SQLite.

Key Features:
Automatic migrations
Relationships support between models
Chainable queries

Hooks for lifecycle events ### 4.2. MongoDB Go Driver
For applications requiring associative or document-based storage, MongoDB's Go driver provides easy access to MongoDB databases from Go applications.

Key Features:
Support for various MongoDB features
Flexible query builder
Aggregation framework support
BSON support for complex data types ## 5. Monitoring and Logging
Monitoring and logging are crucial for microservices to ensure reliability and performance.### 5.1. Prometheus
Prometheus is a powerful monitoring and alerting toolkit designed for cloud-native applications. It's widely used with Go applications to track metrics and provide insights into the system's performance.

Key Features:
Multi-dimensional data model
Powerful query language
Easy integration with Go applications using client libraries
Alerting capabilities### 5.2. Logrus
Logrus is a structured logger for Go that provides flexible logging options. It allows for different log levels and output formats, making it suitable for complex microservices.

Key Features:
Different log levels (info, error, warning, etc.)
Hook support for sending logs to various outputs (file, stdout, etc.)
JSON logging
Extensible functionality through custom hooks ## 6.

Testing Microservices
Testing is an essential aspect of software development, particularly for microservices where individual components need to be verified independently.

6.1. Go Testing Package

The built-in testing package in Go facilitates writing unit tests, benchmarks, and examples. It provides rich support for testing HTTP handlers, making it suitable for testing microservices.

Key Features:
Simple syntax
Integration with Go toolchain
Support for parallel testing
Coverage reports### 6.2. Testify
Testify is a toolkit that provides functionalities such as assertions, mocks, and suite management to enhance the Go testing experience.

Key Features:
Easy assertions for cleaner tests
Mocking capabilities for interfaces
Suite management for organizing related tests

By utilizing the frameworks mentioned above, along with effective service discovery, data management, and monitoring solutions, developers can create robust microservices that are easy to scale and maintain. As the microservices architecture continues to evolve, the Go ecosystem will increasingly provide the necessary tools and frameworks to support developers in their journeys to build resilient and high-performance applications.

Chapter 3: Go Fundamentals for Microservices

In this chapter, we will explore the Go programming language (often referred to as Golang) and its fundamental features that are particularly advantageous for building microservices. We will cover Go's design principles, its concurrency model, essential libraries, and practical examples to help you get started with microservices in Go.

Introduction to Go

Go was developed at Google in the late 2000s and publicly announced in 2012. It was designed to address shortcomings in other programming languages, specifically concerning development speed and ease of use in large-scale software projects. Go is a statically typed, compiled language known for its simplicity and high performance. Some key features that make Go suitable for microservices include:

Concurrent Programming: Go's goroutines and channels make it easy to write concurrent applications, a crucial feature for microservices communicating simultaneously.

Strong Standard Library: Go offers a robust standard library for common tasks, such as HTTP servers, JSON manipulation, and more, minimizing dependency on third-party libraries.

Simplicity and Readability: The concise syntax and

design principles of Go encourage writing clean, maintainable code.

Efficiency: Go compiles to machine code, resulting in fast execution times, which is vital for microservice performance.

Setting Up Your Go Environment

Before diving into Go's features for microservices, you need to set up your development environment:

Installation: Download and install Go from the official Go website (https://golang.org/dl/). Follow the installation instructions for your operating system.

Setting the GOPATH: The GOPATH is an environment variable that defines the root of your Go workspace. You can set it to a directory of your choice. However, with Go modules, many users now rely less on GOPATH, so ensure your Go version supports modules (Go 1.11+).

Creating Your First Project: You can start a new Go project by creating a directory for your project and initializing it with a module:
```bash
mkdir my-microservicecd my-microservice
go mod init my-microservice
```

Core Go Features for Microservices ### 1. Goroutines and Concurrency
Concurrency in Go is achieved through goroutines, which

are lightweight threads managed by the Go runtime. To start a goroutine, simply prefix a function call with the `go` keyword:

```go
go myFunction()
```

Goroutines are non-blocking and allow you to handle multiple tasks simultaneously, which is perfect for microservices that need to handle numerous incoming requests.

2. Channels for Communication

Channels provide a way for goroutines to communicate with each other. You can create a channel and send or receive messages through it:

```go
ch := make(chan string)

go func() {
ch <- "Hello from goroutine!"
}()

msg := <-ch fmt.Println(msg)
```

In microservices, channels can facilitate communication between different services, allowing them to pass messages efficiently.

3. Building an HTTP Server

Building a simple HTTP server is straightforward in Go. You can use the `net/http` package to set up your microservice's HTTP endpoints:

```go
package main

import ( "fmt" "net/http"
)

func handler(w http.ResponseWriter, r *http.Request) {
fmt.Fprintf(w, "Hello, World!")
}

func main() { http.HandleFunc("/", handler)
http.ListenAndServe(":8080", nil)
}
```

This code initializes an HTTP server that responds with "Hello, World!" when accessed at the root URL. You can expand this framework to implement RESTful services for your microservices.

4. JSON Handling

Microservices often exchange data in JSON format. Go provides the `encoding/json` package, allowing for easy serialization and deserialization of JSON data.

Here's an example of encoding a struct into JSON:

45

```go
import (
"encoding/json""net/http"
)

type Message struct { Text string `json:"text"`
}

func jsonHandler(w http.ResponseWriter, r *http.Request)
{ msg := Message{Text: "Hello, JSON!"}
w.Header().Set("Content-Type", "application/json")
json.NewEncoder(w).Encode(msg)
}
```

5. Error Handling

In Go, error handling is explicit, relying on returned error values rather than exceptions. This encourages developers to handle errors properly, a crucial aspect when working with distributed systems like microservices.

```go
file, err := os.Open("filename.txt")if err != nil {
log.Fatal(err)
}
defer file.Close()
```

Creating a Basic Microservice

Now that we have covered essential Go features, let's combine these elements to create a rudimentary

46

microservice. The following example shows how to build a RESTful API that responds with user data.

Step 1: Define the User Struct

```go
type User struct {
ID      int     `json:"id"`
Name string `json:"name"` Email string `json:"email"`
}
```

Step 2: Create an In-Memory Store

```go
var users = []User{
{ID: 1, Name: "Alice", Email: "alice@example.com"},
{ID: 2, Name: "Bob", Email: "bob@example.com"},
}
```

Step 3: Implement the HTTP Handlers

```go
func getUsers(w http.ResponseWriter, r *http.Request) {
w.Header().Set("Content-Type",         "application/json")
json.NewEncoder(w).Encode(users)
}
```

Step 4: Set Up the Routes

```go

47
```

```
func main() { http.HandleFunc("/users", getUsers)
log.Fatal(http.ListenAndServe(":8080", nil))
}
` ` `
```

Step 5: Test Your Microservice

After running your code, you can test your microservice by sending a request to `http://localhost:8080/users`. The JSON response should include the array of users.

From goroutines and channels for concurrency to a strong HTTP library and JSON handling, Go offers the tools needed to create efficient and robust microservices. As you continue your journey in developing microservices with Go, keep practicing and expanding your understanding of the language and its ecosystem. Future chapters will delve deeper into building secure, scalable, and resilient microservices, leveraging Go's capabilities to the fullest.

Key Features of the Go Language

The Go programming language, often referred to as Golang, was developed by Google and released in 2009. Its design principles and unique features make it one of the most preferred languages for modern software development, particularly in cloud services and distributed systems. This chapter explores the key features of Go that contribute to its growing popularity among developers.

1. Simplicity and Minimalism

One of the most notable aspects of Go is its emphasis on simplicity and minimalism. While many programming languages have become bloated with features over time, Go was designed to be straightforward, enabling developers to understand its syntax and structure quickly. The language has a clean and clear syntax that minimizes cognitive load, allowing developers to focus on solving problems rather than wrestling with complex language rules.

Example:
In Go, a simple "Hello, World!" program consists of just a few lines of code:

```go
package mainimport "fmt"
func main() { fmt.Println("Hello, World!")
}
```

This simplicity enables new developers to become productive quickly, leading to faster development cycles and reduced learning curves.

2. Strong Static Typing

Go is statically typed, meaning that variable types are defined at compile time rather than runtime. This feature promotes type safety, allowing developers to catch errors early in the development process before the code is executed. Strong typing helps maintain a clean and predictable codebase, thus reducing the likelihood of runtime errors that can lead to costly bugs.

Example:
In Go, defining a variable with a specific type ensures that only values of that type can be assigned:

```go
var age int = 30
age = "twenty" // This will result in a compile-time error
```

Such strong type enforcement promotes better code quality and robustness.## 3. Concurrency Support

One of the standout features of Go is its built-in support for concurrency. Concurrency allows developers to write programs that can perform multiple tasks simultaneously, effectively utilizing system resources. Go's concurrency model is based on goroutines and channels, providing a simple and efficient way to handle concurrent tasks.

Goroutines:
Goroutines are lightweight threads managed by the Go runtime. They allow developers to spawn concurrent functions easily.

```go
go func() {
fmt.Println("This runs concurrently!")
}()
```

Channels:
Channels provide a way for goroutines to communicate with one another, enabling safe data exchange without the

complexities of thread management.

```go
ch := make(chan string)go func() {
ch <- "Hello from goroutine"
}()
msg := <-ch fmt.Println(msg)
```

This elegant approach to concurrency makes Go particularly well-suited for building scalable and high-performance applications.

4. Garbage Collection

Go features an efficient garbage collection system that automatically manages memory. Developers do not need to explicitly free memory, significantly reducing the risk of memory leaks and other related issues. The garbage collector runs concurrently with the application, allowing it to manage memory without significant impact on performance.

Performance Considerations:
While garbage collection can introduce some latency, Go's runtime is optimized to minimize these interruptions, making it suitable for high-performance applications.

5. Built-In Tooling

Go comes with a rich set of built-in tools that enhance developer productivity. The Go toolchain includesfeatures for testing, profiling, and documentation generation, simplifying many common tasks associatedwith software development.

Testing:
Go's testing framework allows developers to write and run tests easily, promoting a test-driven development (TDD) approach.

```go
func TestSum(t *testing.T) {

result := Sum(1, 2)if result != 3 {
t.Errorf("Expected 3, got %d", result)
}
}
```

Documentation:
Go automatically generates documentation from comments in the code, making it easier to maintain comprehensive and up-to-date documentation.

6. Cross-Platform Compilation

Another compelling feature of Go is its ability to compile code to standalone binaries for different operatingsystems and architectures. Developers can build executables for Windows, macOS, and Linux from within the same development environment, simplifying the deployment process.

Example:
To compile a Go program for a different OS, developers can

set environment variables before running the build command:

```bash
GOOS=linux GOARCH=amd64 go build myapp.go
```

This flexibility is advantageous for organizations deploying applications across various platforms. ## 7. Comprehensive Standard Library
Go comes with a powerful standard library that encompasses a wide range of packages for performing common tasks, including networking, file handling, and cryptography. This extensive array of built-in packages reduces the need for third-party libraries, speeding up development.

Example:
Using the `net/http` package, developers can easily create a simple web server:

```go
package main

import ( "net/http"
)

func handler(w http.ResponseWriter, r *http.Request) {
w.Write([]byte("Hello, World!"))
}

func main() { http.HandleFunc("/", handler)
http.ListenAndServe(":8080", nil)
```

```
}
```

The Go programming language is designed with an emphasis on simplicity, performance, and concurrency, making it an ideal choice for modern software development. Its strong typing, built-in tooling, garbage collection, and comprehensive standard library empower developers to create efficient, scalable applications.

Essential Go Programming Concepts

Created by Google, it is particularly well-suited for building scalable and high-performance systems, making it an ideal choice for developers working in cloud services, microservices architectures, and concurrent programming environments. In this chapter, we will explore essential Go programming concepts that every developer should understand to effectively utilize this powerful language.

1. Go Basics: Syntax and Structure ### 1.1 The Go Program Structure
At the heart of every Go program lies its syntax and structure. A basic Go program includes a package declaration, import statements, and a main function:

```go
package mainimport "fmt"
func main() { fmt.Println("Hello, World!")
}
```

Package Declaration: Every Go file begins with a package declaration, which determines the package's name and scope.

Imports: Go allows you to import packages, which lets you use functions and types from other parts of the Go ecosystem.

Main Function: The `main` function is the entry point for execution.### 1.2 Variables and Types

Go is statically typed, which means that variable types are known at compile time. Variables can be declared using the `var` keyword or the short declaration operator `:=`.

```go
var age int = 30height := 5.9
name := "John Doe"
```

Common data types in Go include:

Basic Types: `int`, `float64`, `bool`, `string`

Composite Types: Arrays, slices, maps, and structs### 1.3 Control Flow

Go supports standard control flow statements such as `if`, `for`, and `switch`.

```go
for i := 0; i < 10; i++ {
```

```go
fmt.Println(i)
}
```

The `for` loop in Go is versatile. It's the only looping construct, making it both a counter and a range loop.## 2. Functions: First-Class Citizens
2.1 Defining Functions

Functions in Go are first-class citizens, which means you can pass them around as values. You definefunctions using the `func` keyword:

```go
func add(a int, b int) int {return a + b
}
```

2.2 Variadic Functions

Go supports variadic functions, which can accept a variable number of arguments:

```go
func sum(numbers ...int) int {total := 0
for _, number := range numbers {total += number
}
return total
}
```

2.3 Higher-Order Functions

Functions can also return other functions, allowing for powerful functional programming techniques:

```go
func makeAdder(x int) func(int) int {return func(y int) int {
return x + y
}
}
```

3. Pointers and Memory Management ### 3.1 Understanding Pointers
A pointer in Go is a variable that stores the memory address of another variable. This enables you to reference and modify data without copying it:

```go
var x int = 10

var p *int = &x
```

3.2 Using Pointers

Pointers are vital for efficient memory management and prevent unnecessary value copying. You can dereference pointers to access the value they point to:

```go
*p = 20 // Changes the value of x to 20
```

4. Structs and Interfaces: Building Blocks of Go ### 4.1 Structs

Structs are composite data types that group together variables under a single name:

```go
type Person struct {Name string
Age int
}
```

4.2 Interfaces

Interfaces in Go provide a way to specify behavior. A type implements an interface by providing concrete implementations of its methods. This reduces coupling and allows for flexibility:

```go
type Speaker interface {Speak() string
}

type Dog struct{}
func (d Dog) Speak() string {return "Woof!"
}

var s Speaker = Dog{}
```

5. Goroutines and Channels: Concurrency Made Easy
5.1 Goroutines
Go provides built-in support for concurrent programming through goroutines. A goroutine is a lightweight thread

managed by the Go runtime:

```go
go func() {
fmt.Println("This runs concurrently")
}()
```

5.2 Channels

Channels are used for communication between goroutines. You can send and receive values using channels, making synchronization simpler:

```go
ch := make(chan int)

go func() {
ch <- 42 // Send 42 to the channel
}()

value := <-ch // Receive from the channel
```

5.3 Select Statement

The `select` statement allows you to wait on multiple channel operations. It's similar to a `switch`, but for channels:

```go
go select {
case msg1 := <-ch1:fmt.Println(msg1) case msg2 := <-ch2:
fmt.Println(msg2)
```

```
case          <-time.After(1          *          time.Second):
fmt.Println("Timeout!")
}
```

6. Error Handling in Go

Go adopts a unique approach to error handling. Instead of exceptions, functions often return an error value alongside the results. It is the caller's responsibility to check for errors:

```go
result, err := someFunction()if err != nil {
fmt.Println("Error:", err)
}
```

This design promotes explicit error handling and reduces the chances of unexpected crashes.

Understanding these essential concepts lays a solid foundation for working with Go. From its unique handling of concurrency to the powerful type system and robust package management, Go provides developers with powerful tools to build modern applications. As you continue to explore Go and its capabilities, you will find that the simplicity and elegance of the language empower you to solve complex problems effectively. The journey into the Go programming language is just beginning, and these concepts will guide you as you dive deeper into its rich ecosystem.

Chapter 4: Designing Microservices with Go

This chapter delves into the design of microservices using Go, a language that excels in simplicity,concurrency, and performance.

4.1 Understanding Microservices Architecture

Before diving into the specifics of designing microservices with Go, it's crucial to understand what microservices architecture entails. Microservices architecture is a style of software development in which applications are structured as loosely coupled services. This approach contrasts with monolithic architecture,where the entire application is built as a single unit.

Key Characteristics of Microservices:
Independently Deployable: Each microservice can be developed, tested, and deployed independently.
Diverse Technology Stacks: Teams can choose different languages or frameworks best suited for their specific service requirements.
Focused on Business Capabilities: Each service represents a specific business capability or domain.
Enhanced Scalability: Each microservice can be scaled independently based on demand.## 4.2 Why Choose Go for Microservices?
Go, also known as Golang, was developed by Google and is known for its efficiency and performance,making it a suitable choice for building microservices. The language's

built-in support for concurrency, simplicity, and strong typing promotes robust and maintainable code.

Advantages of Using Go:
Concurrency Support: Go provides goroutines and channels, which make concurrent programming straightforward and efficient.
Performance: Go compiles directly to machine code, resulting in fast execution times and low memory usage.
Simple Syntax: The language is easy to learn and read, which reduces the cognitive load on developers.
Strong Standard Library: Go's standard library provides built-in support for networking, HTTP, and RESTful services.

4.3 Key Principles for Designing Microservices

When designing microservices with Go, several principles should be considered to ensure your services are effective, maintainable, and scalable.

4.3.1 Single Responsibility Principle

Each microservice should focus on a single piece of functionality or business capability. This makes it easier to understand, test, and maintain. When designing a microservice, ask yourself: "What is the core business function this service provides?"

4.3.2 API Design

A well-defined API is critical for communication between microservices. Go's built-in support for HTTP makes it straightforward to expose RESTful APIs.

Best Practices for API Design:
Use Meaningful Resource URIs: Structure your URIs logically based on the resources they represent.
Version Your APIs: Use versioning to ensure backwards compatibility as your service evolves.
HTTP Methods: Adhere to the principles of REST—using GET, POST, PUT, DELETE appropriately.### 4.3.3 Data Management
Data management can become complicated in a microservices architecture. Each service should ideally own its data store, preventing dependencies on centralized databases.

Strategies for Data Management:
Database Per Service: Each microservice should manage its own database schema.
Event-Driven Architecture: Use event sourcing or publish-subscribe patterns to keep services in sync.## 4.4 Tools and Frameworks in Go
When creating microservices with Go, several frameworks and libraries can expedite development and enhance capabilities.

4.4.1 Gin and Echo

Gin and Echo are popular web frameworks in Go that simplify the creation of RESTful APIs. They provide routing, middleware support, and JSON serialization, making it easy to build efficient microservices.

4.4.2 gRPC

For microservices that require high-performance communication, gRPC can be a great choice. gRPC is a remote procedure call (RPC) framework that uses HTTP/2 and Protocol Buffers, allowing for efficient communication and service definition.

4.4.3 Docker

Containerization is an essential concept in microservices. Using Docker, you can package your Go microservices into containers, making them portable and easy to deploy across various environments.

4.5 Building Your First Microservice in Go

Let's put theory into practice by building a simple microservice with Go. For this example, we will create a basic user service that handles user information.

Step 1: Set Up Your Go Environment

Ensure you have Go installed. Create a new directory for your project and initialize a new Go module.

```bash
mkdir user-servicecd user-service
go mod init user-service
```

Step 2: Create the User Struct

Define the user structure to hold user data in `main.go`.

```go
package main

type User struct {
ID   string `json:"id"` Name string `json:"name"` Age int
     `json:"age"`
}
```

Step 3: Implement the API

Implement basic CRUD functionalities using the Gin framework.

```go
package main

import (
"github.com/gin-gonic/gin"
)
var users = make(map[string]User)func main() {
r := gin.Default()

r.GET("/users/:id", getUser) r.POST("/users", createUser)
r.PUT("/users/:id", updateUser) r.DELETE("/users/:id",
deleteUser)

r.Run(":8080") // listen and serve on 0.0.0.0:8080
}

func getUser(c *gin.Context) { /* implementation */ } func
createUser(c *gin.Context) { /* implementation */ } func
```

```
updateUser(c *gin.Context) { /* implementation */ }func
deleteUser(c *gin.Context) { /* implementation */ }
```

Step 4: Build and Run Your MicroserviceBuild your
service and run it.
```bash
go build
./user-service
```

Your microservice is now up and running, capable of
handling basic user-related requests.

By adhering to sound design principles and leveraging Go's
features and ecosystem, you can create highly scalable and
maintainable services that effectively meet business needs.
As we move forward, the following chapters will explore
advanced topics, deployment strategies, and best practices
for maintaining a microservices-based application in
production.

Principles of Effective Microservice Design

This paradigm shift emphasizes modularity, scalability,
and resilience, facilitating continuous delivery and
deployment. However, designing effective microservices
requires a deep understanding of several principles that
guide not only the development process but also the
integration, monitoring, and maintenance of these
services. This chapter explores the core principles essential
for effective microservice design, providing a roadmap for
creating systems that are flexible, manageable, and robust.

1. Single Responsibility

At the heart of microservice architecture is the principle of single responsibility. A microservice should encapsulate a specific business capability, ensuring that it has a defined boundary. This approach minimizes coupling, allowing teams to develop, deploy, and scale services independently. For example, if your application includes user management, payment processing, and order fulfillment, these functionalities should be divided into distinct microservices. Each service remains focused and easy to understand, making it simpler to implement changes or enhancements without affecting other parts of the system.

Key Takeaway:
Design microservices to focus on a single business capability to enhance maintainability and reduce complexity.

2. Autonomy

Each microservice should be autonomous and self-sufficient. This autonomy means that microservices should manage their own data store, business logic, and service dependencies. When a service is autonomous, it can operate independently of others, facilitating continuous integration and delivery (CI/CD). For instance, if a shipping service needs to retrieve data from an inventory service, it should do so without being tightly coupled to it. Instead, the shipping service should handle its own data logic and utilize APIs or message queues for communication.

Key Takeaway:
Strive for microservices that are autonomous to promote independent deployment and operational efficiency. ## 3. Domain-Driven Design

Embracing domain-driven design (DDD) principles can significantly enhance microservices architecture. DDD encourages the alignment of microservices with business domains, ensuring that microservices reflect actual business processes and terminology. This practice requires collaboration between domain experts and developers to identify bounded contexts, or areas of responsibility within the system. By organizing services around business capabilities, teams can create clear boundaries and responsibilities, which facilitates scalability and enhances the overall comprehensibility of the system.

Key Takeaway:
Utilize domain-driven design to create microservices that align closely with business domains and processes. ## 4. Communication Strategies

Effective communication between microservices is crucial for a successful architecture. Microservices often communicate through APIs, typically using REST or gRPC for synchronous communication or message brokers (like Kafka or RabbitMQ) for asynchronous communication.

The choice of communication strategy can greatly impact system performance, resilience, and complexity. For instance, while RESTful APIs are easy to implement and widely adopted, using asynchronous messaging can decouple services, reducing bottlenecks and enhancing the system's fault tolerance.

Key Takeaway:
Choose an appropriate communication strategy based on the needs of the system and the use cases of the microservices.

5. Decentralized Data Management

In a microservice architecture, each service should manage its own database or storage mechanism. This decentralization is a core principle that enhances data integrity and scalability. However, this can lead to challenges related to data consistency and coordination across services. Employ patterns such as event sourcing or the saga pattern to help manage distributed transactions and ensure data synchronization. By decentralizing data management, teams can make technology choices that best suit the specific needs of each service.

Key Takeaway:
Encourage decentralized data management to promote service independence and avoid tight coupling of data.

6. Resilience and Fault Tolerance

Microservices must be resilient and fault-tolerant to cope with failures gracefully. By building in resilience, services can respond to flaws without disrupting the entire system. Implement circuit breakers, retries, and fallbacks to manage failures effectively. Designing for failure also involves implementing health checks and monitoring systems to detect issues early. For example, using tools like Hystrix for circuit breaking allows services to degrade gracefully when dependencies fail, thus maintaining availability and responsiveness.

Key Takeaway:
Prepare for potential failures by implementing resilience and fault-tolerant strategies in microservices. ## 7. Observability and Monitoring
With multiple microservices interacting, it is critical to implement robust observability and monitoring strategies. Effective logging, tracing, and metrics collection provide insight into service performance, user interactions, and system health. Tools like Prometheus for metrics, Grafana for dashboards, and OpenTelemetry for distributed tracing can help teams visualize the state of microservices and identify bottlenecks or failures quickly. By fostering observability, organizations can enhance incident response and improve overall system reliability.

Key Takeaway:
Establish comprehensive monitoring and observability practices to maintain service health and performance.

By adhering to these principles—single responsibility, autonomy, domain-driven design, communication strategies, decentralized data management, resilience, and observability—development teams can craft microservices architectures that are scalable, maintainable, and adaptable to changing business needs. As organizations continue to embrace microservices, applying these foundational principles will be essential to achieving success in their software development endeavors.

Structuring Go Code for Scalability

As systems grow and user demand increases, the structure of the codebase becomes crucial to maintaining performance, manageability, and extensibility. Go, also known as Golang, is a statically typed language designed for efficiency and scalability. This chapter delves into best practices for structuring Go code to ensure that it is primed for scalability from the outset.

1. Understanding Scalability

Before we dive into structuring techniques, let's clarify what scalability means in the context of Go and software architecture in general. Scalability refers to a system's ability to handle a growing amount of work or its potential to be enlarged to accommodate that growth. When structuring Go code, we must consider both vertical and horizontal scalability:

Vertical Scalability: This involves adding more resources (CPU, memory) to the existing server or instances to enhance performance.

Horizontal Scalability: This method involves adding more instances to the service, such as deploying multiple services across servers or containers.

In Go, the built-in support for concurrency via goroutines and channels makes it an excellent candidate for building scalable applications.

2. Project Structure

A well-defined project structure is the foundation for scalable Go applications. Organizing your Go project effectively promotes clarity and fosters collaboration. The following approaches can be utilized:

2.1. Use a Standard Directory Layout

Adopting a standard directory layout, such as the "Standard Go Project Layout," helps developers navigate the project effortlessly. A suggested structure might look like:

```
/myappcmd
myapp          # Application entry point
internal       # Private application and library code
serviceA
serviceB
pkg            # Library code intended for use by external
applicationsapi     # API definitions, gRPC/protobuf
files, etc.
configs        # Configuration files
scripts# Deployment scripts
test    # Test data and third-party services
```

This structure keeps your application organized while allowing teams to work on different components concurrently without stepping on each other's toes.

2.2. Modular Design

72

Go encourages a modular design that breaks down applications into smaller, independently deployable services. By using interfaces, you can define clear contracts between components, which allows for easier testing and flexibility in implementation. When you adhere to the principles of modularity, you can swap out services or components with minimal disruption.

2.3. Isolation of Concerns

Following the principle of Separation of Concerns (SoC) allows you to keep different functionalities distinct. For example, separate your business logic, data access patterns, and API handling into different packages or modules. This separation not only simplifies maintenance but also enhances testability and scalability.

3. Concurrency Patterns

Go's concurrency model, based on goroutines and channels, makes it a breeze to write concurrent code. To fully leverage Go's concurrency features, consider the following patterns:

3.1. Worker Pools

Using worker pools allows you to control concurrency efficiently. This design pattern involves creating a fixed number of worker goroutines that receive tasks from a shared job queue. It can prevent your application from overwhelming resources during peak load times.

```go
func worker(jobs <-chan Job, wg *sync.WaitGroup) {defer
wg.Done()
for job := range jobs {process(job)
}
}
```

3.2. Rate Limiting

When building scalable applications, it's important to control the rate at which certain actions are executed, especially when dealing with external APIs or services. Implementing rate-limiting mechanisms can protect your application from being throttled or banned and ensure consistent performance.

```go
limiter := time.NewTicker(100 * time.Millisecond) // Allow one job every 100 msdefer limiter.Stop()

for job := range jobs {
<-limiter.C process(job)
}
```

3.3. Context Management

Go provides the `context` package to handle cancellation signals and deadlines across API boundaries. Using contexts correctly can prevent resource leaks and ensure your application scales without accumulating excess memory usage due to lingering goroutines.

4. Configuration Management

As applications grow, configuration management becomes vital. Use environment variables or configuration files to manage different environments (development, testing, production). This approach makes your application flexible and promotes scalability as you can adapt configurations without code changes.

```go
type Config struct {
Port   string `env:"PORT"` Debug bool `env:"DEBUG"`
}
```

5. Testing and CI/CD

A scalable Go application must also incorporate robust testing and Continuous Integration/Continuous Deployment (CI/CD) practices. Implement unit tests and integration tests that verify the behavior of various components. Use frameworks like `Go test` and CI/CD tools like GitHub Actions, GitLab CI, or Jenkins to automate your testing and deployment processes.

6. Monitoring and Profiling

Lastly, to maintain scalability, you must have an effective strategy for monitoring and profiling your applications. Implement logging and use monitoring tools like Prometheus or Grafana to visualize performance metrics. Profiling tools can also help identify performance bottlenecks, allowing for timelyoptimizations.

By employing a disciplined project structure, leveraging concurrency patterns, managing configurations effectively, and incorporating a solid testing pipeline, you ensure that your Go applications will not only perform well under load but also remain maintainable and adaptable as your user base grows. Embrace theseprinciples, and you will set a solid foundation for future growth and success in your Go programming endeavors.

]

Chapter 5: Building Your First Microservice

By breaking down a large monolithic application into smaller, independent services, we can achieve greater agility, scalability, and maintainability. In this chapter, we will walk through the process of building your first microservice using the Go programming language (Golang). We'll cover everything from setting up your development environment to deploying your microservice.

5.1 Introduction to Go

Go, also known as Golang, is a statically typed, compiled programming language designed at Google. It isknown for its simplicity, efficiency, and strong support for concurrent programming. These features makeGo an excellent choice for building microservices.

Benefits of Using Go for Microservices

Performance: Being a compiled language, Go offers great performance, making it suitable for high-performance applications.

Concurrency: Go's goroutines and channels provide elegant solutions for handling concurrent operations, which is essential for scalable microservices.

Strongly Typed: Go's type system reduces the likelihood of runtime errors, enhancing the reliabilityof your services.

Standard Library: Go's rich standard library simplifies web server creation, API interactions, and data manipulation.

Community Support: An extensive community provides numerous libraries and frameworks, making development easier.

5.2 Setting Up Your Development Environment

Before we start coding, we need to set up our development environment.### 5.2.1 Installing Go
Download the Go installation package from the [official website](https://golang.org/dl/).
Follow the installation instructions for your operating system (Windows, macOS, or Linux).
After installation, verify it by running:

```bash
go version
```

5.2.2 Setting Up Your Workspace

Create a workspace directory for your Go projects. The typical structure looks like this:

```
~/go/
src/
yourproject/
```

```
bin/
```

You may also want to set the `GOPATH` environment variable to point to your workspace directory.

```bash
export GOPATH=~/go
```

5.2.3 Installing Necessary Tools

We will use some essential tools for development:

HTTP Router: `gorilla/mux` is a powerful URL router and dispatcher for Go. Install it via:

```bash
go get -u github.com/gorilla/mux
```

JSON Handling: Go's standard library has great support for JSON. ## 5.3 Creating Your First Microservice Let's create a simple microservice that provides a RESTful API for managing a list of tasks. Each task will have an ID, a title, and a completion status.

5.3.1 Project Structure

First, create the project directory and structure it as follows:

```
```

```
~/go/src/task-service/main.go
task.go
```

5.3.2 Defining the Task Model In `task.go`, define the `Task` model:

```go
package main

type Task struct {
ID      string `json:"id"` Title      string `json:"title"`
Completed bool  `json:"completed"`
}

var tasks []Task
```

5.3.3 Implementing Handlers

In `main.go`, implement the HTTP handlers for our microservice.

```go
package main

import ( "encoding/json""net/http"
"github.com/gorilla/mux"
)

func getTasks(w http.ResponseWriter, r *http.Request) {
w.Header().Set("Content-Type",      "application/json")
json.NewEncoder(w).Encode(tasks)
}
```

```go
func createTask(w http.ResponseWriter, r *http.Request) {
	var task Task
	json.NewDecoder(r.Body).Decode(&task)    tasks    =
	append(tasks, task) w.WriteHeader(http.StatusCreated)
	json.NewEncoder(w).Encode(task)
}

func main() {
	router := mux.NewRouter()
	router.HandleFunc("/tasks", getTasks).Methods("GET")
	router.HandleFunc("/tasks",
	createTask).Methods("POST")

	http.ListenAndServe(":8000", router)
}
```

5.3.4 Running the Microservice

Open your terminal and navigate to the `task-service` directory.
Run the following command to start the service:

```bash
go run main.go task.go
```

Your microservice should now be running on `http://localhost:8000`.## 5.4 Testing the Microservice
To test our API, you can use tools like `curl` or Postman.
5.4.1 Adding a Task
Use the following command to add a new task:

```bash
curl -X POST http://localhost:8000/tasks -d '{"id":"1",
"title":"Learn Go", "completed":false}' -H "Content-Type:
application/json"
```

5.4.2 Retrieving All TasksTo retrieve all tasks, run:
```bash
curl http://localhost:8000/tasks
```

In this chapter, we explored the advantages of using Go for microservices, set up our development environment, and created a simple task management API. This foundational knowledge will serve you well as you continue to build and scale microservices. In the next chapter, we will delve into advanced topics such as database integration, error handling, and testing your microservices effectively. Happy coding!

Writing a Basic Go Microservice

Microservices architecture is a modern software development practice that structures an application as a collection of loosely coupled services. Each service is designed to handle a specific business capability and can be developed, deployed, and scaled independently. The Go programming language, known for its performance, simplicity, and powerful concurrency support, is an excellent choice for writing microservices.In this chapter, we will build a basic Go microservice step by step.

Setting Up Your Go Environment

Before we start writing our microservice, ensure that you have the Go programming language installed on your machine. You can download the latest version from the official Go website: golang.org/dl.

Once installed, you can verify your installation by running:

```bash
go version
```

You should see a response indicating the installed version of Go.### Create a Project Directory
Next, we will create a new directory for our microservice project. Open your terminal and run the following commands:

```bash
mkdir go-microservicecd go-microservice
go mod init go-microservice
```

The `go mod init` command initializes a new Go module, which will help to manage dependencies.## Writing the Microservice
Step 1: Define the Service

Let's create a simple microservice that serves as a todo list. We want users to be able to create, retrieve, anddelete their todo items. Create a new file called `main.go` in your project directory:

```bash
touch main.go
```

Open `main.go` and start by importing the necessary packages:

```go
package main

import ( "encoding/json""net/http" "sync"
)
```

Step 2: Create Todo Structure

Next, we will define a struct to represent our todo items:

```go
type Todo struct {
ID string `json:"id"` Task string `json:"task"`
}
```

We will also need a slice to store our todos and a mutex to handle concurrent access:

```go
var (
todos = []Todo{} mu sync.Mutex nextID = 1
)
```

Step 3: Implement Handlers

Now, we will create the HTTP handlers for our microservice. Below, we will implement three handlers: `createTodo`, `getTodos`, and `deleteTodo`.

```go
func createTodo(w http.ResponseWriter, r *http.Request)
{var todo Todo
if err := json.NewDecoder(r.Body).Decode(&todo); err !=
nil {http.Error(w, err.Error(), http.StatusBadRequest)
return
}

mu.Lock()
todo.ID = fmt.Sprintf("%d", nextID)nextID++
todos = append(todos, todo)mu.Unlock()

w.WriteHeader(http.StatusCreated)
json.NewEncoder(w).Encode(todo)
}

func getTodos(w http.ResponseWriter, r *http.Request) {
mu.Lock()
defer mu.Unlock()

w.WriteHeader(http.StatusOK)
json.NewEncoder(w).Encode(todos)
}

func deleteTodo(w http.ResponseWriter, r *http.Request)
{id := r.URL.Query().Get("id")
```

```go
    mu.Lock()
    defer mu.Unlock()

    for i, todo := range todos {if todo.ID == id {
    todos       =        append(todos[:i],        todos[i+1:]...)
    w.WriteHeader(http.StatusNoContent) return
    }
    }
    http.Error(w, "Todo not found", http.StatusNotFound)
    }
```

Step 4: Set Up the Router

In the `main` function, you will set up a router and define the endpoints:

```go
func main() {
http.HandleFunc("/todos", createTodo).Methods("POST")
http.HandleFunc("/todos",    getTodos).Methods("GET")
http.HandleFunc("/todos",
deleteTodo).Methods("DELETE")

http.ListenAndServe(":8080", nil)
}
```

Step 5: Testing the Microservice

To test your microservice, you can use tools like `curl` or Postman. Start your Go server in the terminal:

```bash
go run main.go
```

You can create, retrieve, and delete todo items using the following commands:

Create a new todo:
```bash
curl -X POST http://localhost:8080/todos -d '{"task": "Learn Go"}' -H 'Content-Type: application/json'
```

Get all todos:
```bash
curl http://localhost:8080/todos
```

Delete a todo (replace `<ID>` with the actual ID):
```bash
curl -X DELETE http://localhost:8080/todos?id=<ID>
```

We covered setting up the Go environment, defining a Todo struct, implementing HTTP handlers, and testing the microservice. With Go's efficient concurrency model and ease of use, you can scale this microservice further by introducing features such as persistence with a database or implementing authentication. The principles learned here can be applied to develop high-performance microservices in any domain.

Running and Testing Your Service

In this chapter, we will explore the intricacies of running your Go service, monitoring its performance, and implementing effective testing strategies. We'll cover topics such as the Go runtime environment, logging, error handling, and the various types of tests you can implement to ensure the robustness of your application.

1. Setting Up Your Go Environment

Before running your service, ensure that you have a suitable environment:

1.1 Installing Go

If you haven't installed Go yet, download it from the [official Go website](https://golang.org/dl/) and follow the installation instructions specific to your operating system (Windows, macOS, or Linux). After the installation, confirm that it was successful by running the following command in your terminal:

```bash
go version
```

This command will output the installed version of Go. ### 1.2 Structuring Your Project
A well-structured project is essential for running and testing effectively. The common Go project structure includes:

```
/your-servicecmd
your-servicemain.go
internalpkg tests go.mod
```

Here, `/cmd` contains the main application entry points, `/internal` houses private application code, `/pkg` can host shared libraries, and `/tests` is where you'll place your test cases.

2. Running Your Service

Once your service is ready, it's time to run it. ### 2.1 Running a Simple Service
Go offers a straightforward command to run your service. Navigate to your service's directory and execute:

```bash
go run cmd/your-service/main.go
```

This will compile and execute your main application. You should see output indicating that your service is running, following any logs you've added.

2.2 Build and Deploy

When you're ready to share your application, you can build a binary executable using:

```bash
```

```
go build -o your-service ./cmd/your-service
```

This command generates a binary that you can deploy on your server or share with others. To run the binary, simply execute:

```bash
./your-service
```

2.3 Running with Environment Variables

If your service relies on environment variables, you can set them before running your application:

```bash
export LISTEN_ADDRESS=:8080
go run cmd/your-service/main.go
```

Using environment variables enhances configurability and sets different environments (development, staging, production) easily.

3. Logging and Monitoring

A robust logging and monitoring system is crucial for diagnosing issues:### 3.1 Implementing Logging
Go's `log` package offers simple logging capabilities:

```go
import "log"
```

```
func main() { log.Println("Service starting...")
// Your service code here
}
```
```

For more advanced logging, consider using packages like `logrus` or `zap`, which provide structured logging and additional features.

### 3.2 Monitoring Your Service

Monitor your application during runtime to ensure performance reliability. Implement health check endpoints (`/health` or `/status`) that can return the current state of the service.

### 3.3 Performance Metrics

Integrate tools like Prometheus to collect metrics (CPU, memory usage, request latency) and visualize them using Dashboards like Grafana.

## 4. Testing Your Service

Testing your service is essential to maintain code quality and performance. Go's built-in testing framework makes it easy to implement various types of tests.

### 4.1 Unit Testing

Create a test file alongside your service code. For example, if your code resides in `service.go`, create
```

`service_test.go`:

```go
package yourserviceimport "testing"
func TestFunctionName(t *testing.T) { result :=
FunctionName()
expected := "expectedValue"

if result != expected {
t.Errorf("Expected %v, got %v", expected, result)
}
}
```

Run your tests with:

```bash
go test ./...
```

4.2 Integration Testing

Integration tests verify the interaction between different parts of your application. They typically involve external components such as databases. Use Docker Compose to run an isolated test environment.

4.3 Benchmark Testing

Benchmark tests help to measure the performance of specific functions. In your test file, add a benchmark function:

```go
func BenchmarkFunctionName(b *testing.B) {for i := 0; i <
b.N; i++ {
FunctionName()
}
}
```

Run the benchmarks with:

```bash
go test -bench=.
```

By understanding how to structure your project, execute
the service, implement logging and monitoring, and create
unit and integration tests, you can ensure that your
application remains robust and reliable. In the next
chapter, we will delve into advanced topics, including API
design and versioning strategies. Happy coding!

Chapter 6: Communication Between Microservices

In the realm of microservices architecture, effective communication between services is crucial for a seamless and scalable application. As systems grow in complexity, the need to coordinate between independent services becomes paramount. In this chapter, we will explore various communication strategies between microservices using the Go programming language, examining both synchronous and asynchronous approaches and their respective advantages and trade-offs.

6.1 Overview of Communication Strategies

Microservices can communicate through various protocols and patterns. The most common methods include:

RESTful APIs: A widely-used approach that leverages HTTP for communication. Services expose endpoints that can be consumed by other services or clients.
gRPC: A high-performance RPC framework developed by Google that uses HTTP/2 and Protocol Buffers for serialization, providing advantages such as bidirectional streaming and built-in authentication.
Message Brokers: Asynchronous communication through message brokers (e.g., RabbitMQ, Kafka) enables decoupling services and allows scalability.
GraphQL: An alternative to traditional REST APIs, providing flexibility in querying data across services.

We will delve deeper into these methods, exploring how to

implement them in Go.## 6.2 RESTful Communication
6.2.1 Building a RESTful API in Go

Go's `net/http` package makes it easy to create a RESTful API. Below is a simple example of setting up a RESTful service.

```go
package main

import ( "encoding/json""net/http"
)

type Message struct { ID    int    `json:"id"`
Content string `json:"content"`
}

var messages []Message

func    getMessages(w    http.ResponseWriter,    r
*http.Request)    {    w.Header().Set("Content-Type",
"application/json")
json.NewEncoder(w).Encode(messages)
}

func    createMessage(w    http.ResponseWriter,    r
*http.Request)    {    var    message    Message
json.NewDecoder(r.Body).Decode(&message)
messages    =    append(messages,    message)
w.WriteHeader(http.StatusCreated)
}

func main() {
```

95

```go
    http.HandleFunc("/messages",              getMessages)
    http.HandleFunc("/messages/create",     createMessage)
    http.ListenAndServe(":8080", nil)
}
```

6.2.2 Consuming a RESTful API

To consume a RESTful API, you can use `http.NewRequest` and `http.Client`. Here's how you can fetch messages from our previous service:

```go
func fetchMessages() ([]Message, error) {
resp, err := http.Get("http://localhost:8080/messages")if err != nil {
return nil, err
}
defer resp.Body.Close()

var messages []Message
err = json.NewDecoder(resp.Body).Decode(&messages)
return messages, err
}
```

6.2.3 Error Handling

Proper error handling is crucial in any communication mechanism. For instance, when consuming a REST API, you should check the response's status code and handle errors appropriately.

6.3 gRPC Communication ### 6.3.1 Setting Up gRPC

gRPC is an excellent choice for high-performance communication between microservices. Below are the steps to set up a basic gRPC service in Go.

6.3.1.1 Defining the Service

You'll start by defining your service using Protocol Buffers (proto files):

```protobuf
syntax = "proto3";package messages;

service Messenger {
rpc SendMessage (Message) returns (Response);
}

message Message {string content = 1;
}

message Response {bool success = 1;
}
```

6.3.1.2 Generating Code

Use the `protoc` compiler to generate Go code from your protobuf file:

```bash
protoc --go_out=. --go-grpc_out=. messages.proto
```

6.3.1.3 Implementing the Service Now, implement the service in Go:

```go
package main

import ( "context""log"
"net"

pb "path/to/messages" "google.golang.org/grpc"
)

type server struct { pb.UnimplementedMessengerServer
}

func (s *server) SendMessage(ctx context.Context, msg *pb.Message) (*pb.Response, error) {log.Printf("Received message: %s", msg.Content)
return &pb.Response{Success: true}, nil
}

func main() {
lis, err := net.Listen("tcp", ":50051")if err != nil {
log.Fatalf("failed to listen: %v", err)
}
grpcServer                   :=                   grpc.NewServer()
pb.RegisterMessengerServer(grpcServer,        &server{})
grpcServer.Serve(lis)
```

```
}
```

6.3.2 Consuming a gRPC Service

To call the gRPC service from a client, you would set it up
as follows:

```go
package main

import ( "context""log"
"time"

pb "path/to/messages" "google.golang.org/grpc"
)

func sendMessage(content string) {
conn,      err      :=      grpc.Dial("localhost:50051",
grpc.WithInsecure())if err != nil {
log.Fatalf("did not connect: %v", err)
}
defer conn.Close()

client := pb.NewMessengerClient(conn)
ctx, cancel := context.WithTimeout(context.Background(),
time.Second)defer cancel()

response,      err      :=      client.SendMessage(ctx,
&pb.Message{Content: content})if err != nil {
log.Fatalf("could not send message: %v", err)
}
log.Printf("Message sent: %v", response.Success)
```

```
}
```

6.4 Asynchronous Communication with Message Brokers

As microservices grow, scalability and resilience become critical. Asynchronous messaging, using systems like RabbitMQ or Apache Kafka, allows services to communicate without coupling them directly.

6.4.1 RabbitMQ Example #### 6.4.1.1 Sending a Message
To send a message to a RabbitMQ queue:

```go
package main

import ( "github.com/streadway/amqp"

"log"
)

func sendMessage() {
conn,                          err                          :=
amqp.Dial("amqp://guest:guest@localhost:5672/") if  err
!= nil {
log.Fatalf("Failed to connect: %s", err)
}
defer conn.Close()

ch, err := conn.Channel()if err != nil {
log.Fatalf("Failed to open a channel: %s", err)
```

```go
}
defer ch.Close()

err = ch.Publish( "",          // exchange
"hello", // queue name false, // mandatory false, //
immediate amqp.Publishing{
ContentType: "text/plain",
Body: []byte("Hello World!"),
})
if err != nil {
log.Fatalf("Failed to publish a message: %s", err)
}
}
```

6.4.1.2 Receiving a Message

To consume messages from the RabbitMQ queue:

```go
func consumeMessages() {
conn,                          err                          :=
amqp.Dial("amqp://guest:guest@localhost:5672/") if  err
!= nil {
log.Fatalf("Failed to connect: %s", err)
}
defer conn.Close()

ch, err := conn.Channel()if err != nil {
log.Fatalf("Failed to open a channel: %s", err)
}
defer ch.Close()
```

```go
msgs, err := ch.Consume("hello", // queue name "",   //
consumer true,                   // auto-ack

false, // exclusivefalse, // no-local false, // no-wait nil,
     // args
)
if err != nil {
log.Fatalf("Failed to register a consumer: %s", err)
}

for msg := range msgs {
log.Printf("Received a message: %s", msg.Body)
}
}
```
```

Effective communication between microservices is vital for a robust architecture. In this chapter, we explored various methods to facilitate this communication in Go, including RESTful APIs, gRPC, andmessage brokers. Each method comes with its own set of advantages and scenarios for optimal usage.

As you design your microservices, consider the interactions between them. Your choice of communicationmethod will depend on the specific needs of your application, regarding factors like performance, complexity, scalability, and maintainability. Understanding these patterns will empower you to build more resilient and agile microservices.
```

Implementing RESTful APIs in Go

They provide a flexible and scalable way to structure communication between different parts of a system, whether it be client-server architecture, microservices, or integrations with third-party applications. Go, a statically typed, compiled language designed for simplicity and efficiency, is an excellent choice for implementing RESTful APIs. This chapter will guide you through the process of designing and building aRESTful API using Go, exploring its core packages, best practices, and common pitfalls.

Understanding RESTful Concepts

Before diving into implementation, it's essential to understand the core concepts of RESTful APIs:

Resources: In REST, everything is treated as a resource, identified by a unique URI (Uniform Resource Identifier). For example, a user resource might be represented by `/users`.

HTTP Methods: RESTful APIs leverage standard HTTP methods to perform operations on resources:
GET: Retrieve a resource or collection of resources.
POST: Create a new resource.
PUT/PATCH: Update an existing resource.
DELETE: Remove a resource.

Statelessness: Each request from a client contains all the necessary information to process that request. The server does not store any client context between requests.

HATEOAS (Hypermedia as the Engine of Application State): Clients interact with the API through hypermedia links provided by the server, which allows for a more dynamic and flexible API.

Setting Up the Go Environment

To begin, you'll need to set up your Go environment if you haven't already:

Install Go: Download Go from the [official website](https://golang.org/dl/) and follow the installationinstructions.

Set Up Your Workspace: Create a project directory for your API, something like `go-rest-api`, and navigate into it.

Initialize a Go Module: Run the command:
```bash
go mod init go-rest-api
```

Building Your First RESTful API ### Directory Structure
Before writing code, it helps to plan a basic directory structure. A simple example might look like this:

```
/go-rest-apimain.go
```

```
handlers/user.go
models/
user.go
```

Defining the User Model

In `models/user.go`, define a simple user structure:

```go
package models

type User struct {
ID      string `json:"id"` Name string `json:"name"` Email
string `json:"email"`
}
```

Creating Handlers

Next, implement the API handlers in `handlers/user.go`.
Below is an example of a basic user handler:

```go
package handlers

import ( "encoding/json""net/http" "sync"

"go-rest-api/models"
)

var (
users = make(map[string]models.User)mutex sync.Mutex
```

```go
)

func GetUsers(w http.ResponseWriter, r *http.Request) {
mutex.Lock()
defer mutex.Unlock()

w.Header().Set("Content-Type",          "application/json")
json.NewEncoder(w).Encode(users)
}

func CreateUser(w http.ResponseWriter, r *http.Request)
{var user models.User
err := json.NewDecoder(r.Body).Decode(&user)if err != nil
{
http.Error(w, err.Error(), http.StatusBadRequest)return

}

mutex.Lock() users[user.ID] = usermutex.Unlock()

w.WriteHeader(http.StatusCreated)
json.NewEncoder(w).Encode(user)
}
```

Main Function

In your `main.go`, set up the HTTP server and define routes:

```go
package main
```

```go
import ( "log" "net/http"

"go-rest-api/handlers"
)

func main() {
http.HandleFunc("/users",              handlers.GetUsers)
http.HandleFunc("/users/create", handlers.CreateUser)

log.Println("Starting server on :8080")
if err := http.ListenAndServe(":8080", nil); err != nil {
log.Fatal(err)
}
}
```

Running the API

To run your API, execute the following command in your terminal:

```bash
go run main.go
```

Your RESTful API should now be accessible at `http://localhost:8080`. You can use tools like Postman or CURL to send requests and interact with your API.

Testing Your API

To test your API, you can use cURL or Postman. Here are some example commands:

Create a User:

```bash
curl -X POST http://localhost:8080/users/create \

-H "Content-Type: application/json" \
-d '{"id": "1", "name": "Jane Doe", "email": "jane@example.com"}'
```

Get Users:

```bash
curl http://localhost:8080/users
```

Error Handling and Response Formatting

Implementing robust error handling and standardized response formats are crucial for a production-readyAPI.

Error Handling

To improve error handling, you might create a struct that standardizes responses:

```go
type ErrorResponse struct { Message string
`json:"message"`Code int `json:"code"`
}
```

You can use it to format error responses in your handlers, ensuring uniformity.### Middleware
Adding middleware can enhance your API's functionality by handling cross-cutting concerns, such as logging, authentication, or CORS. You can create a simple logging middleware as follows:

```go
func loggingMiddleware(next http.Handler) http.Handler {
return http.HandlerFunc(func(w http.ResponseWriter, r *http.Request) {log.Printf("Request: %s %s", r.Method, r.URL.Path) next.ServeHTTP(w, r)
})
}
```

While this example is foundational, there's a vast array of functionalities and optimizations that can be applied, such as integrating a database, implementing authentication, and more complex routing. Go's simplicity, performance, and strong standard library make it a compelling choice for developing robust, scalable APIs. As you dive deeper, keep refining your understanding of Go's concurrency model, testing capabilities, and ecosystem libraries that enhance API development. With these tools, you can create efficient, reliable RESTful services that stand the test of scale and complexity.

Exploring gRPC for High-Performance Communication

With its simplicity, speed, and support for multiple programming languages, gRPC enables developers to build powerful applications with high-performance communication. This chapter explores gRPC within the Go programming language (often referred to as Golang), investigating its features, benefits, and practical implementation strategies.

Understanding gRPC

gRPC is built on HTTP/2, which allows for multiplexing multiple requests over a single connection, reducing latency and improving throughput. It employs Protocol Buffers (protobufs) as its interface definition language (IDL), enabling developers to define the structure of the data exchanged between services efficiently. The combination of HTTP/2 and Protocol Buffers ensures that gRPC is not only fast but also flexible and cross-platform.

Key Features of gRPC

Multiplexed Connections: gRPC leverages HTTP/2 to support multiple concurrent streams over a single TCP connection, reducing overhead associated with establishing multiple connections.

Efficient Serialization: Protocol Buffers are a compact binary format that allows for efficient data serialization and deserialization, which is crucial for high-performance communication.

Streaming: gRPC supports bi-directional streaming, enabling clients and servers to send and receive messages in real-time. This feature is particularly beneficial for applications requiring continuous data flow, such as video streaming or chat applications.

Language-Agnostic: While gRPC has a strong support base in Go, it also supports numerous programming languages, allowing for seamless communication between services written in different languages.

Error Handling: gRPC provides a rich set of error codes that can be returned to the client, making it easier to implement robust error handling mechanisms.

Setting Up gRPC in Go

To utilize gRPC in a Go application, developers need to follow a structured approach to set up their services. This section outlines the steps to create a basic gRPC service in Go.

Step 1: Install gRPC and Protocol Buffers

Before diving into coding, you need to install the necessary packages. In your Go project directory, run:

```bash
go get google.golang.org/grpc
go get google.golang.org/protobuf
```

```
```

Additionally, ensure that you have Protocol Buffers installed on your system. You can download the protocol buffer compiler (protoc) from the [official Protocol Buffers release page](https://github.com/protocolbuffers/protobuf/releases).

Step 2: Define the Service

Create a `.proto` file to define your gRPC service and the messages it will use. For example, let's create a simple echo service.

```protobuf
syntax = "proto3";package echo;
service EchoService {
rpc Echo(EchoRequest) returns (EchoResponse);
}

message EchoRequest {string message = 1;
}

message EchoResponse {string message = 1;
}
```

Step 3: Generate Go Code from the Proto File

Run the following command to generate the Go code from your `.proto` file:

```bash
protoc --go_out=. --go-grpc_out=. echo.proto
```

This command generates two files: one for message types and another for the gRPC client and serverinterfaces.

Step 4: Implement the Server

Create a server implementation for the defined service:

```go
package main

import ( "context""log"
"net"

pb "path/to/your/generated/proto/file" // Update with your actual path"google.golang.org/grpc"
)

type server struct { pb.UnimplementedEchoServiceServer
}

func (s *server) Echo(ctx context.Context, req *pb.EchoRequest) (*pb.EchoResponse, error) { return &pb.EchoResponse{Message: req.Message}, nil
}

func main() {
lis, err := net.Listen("tcp", ":50051")if err != nil {
log.Fatalf("failed to listen: %v", err)
}
```

```go
grpcServer                   :=                    grpc.NewServer()
pb.RegisterEchoServiceServer(grpcServer, &server{})

log.Println("Server is running on port 50051") if err :=
grpcServer.Serve(lis); err != nil {
log.Fatalf("failed to serve: %v", err)
}
}
```

Step 5: Implement the Client

Now, create a client that can call the echo service:

```go
package main

import ( "context""log"
"time"

pb "path/to/your/generated/proto/file" // Update with
your actual path"google.golang.org/grpc"
)

func main() {
conn,      err      :=       grpc.Dial("localhost:50051",
grpc.WithInsecure(),                     grpc.WithBlock(),
grpc.WithTimeout(5*time.Second))
if err != nil {
log.Fatalf("did not connect: %v", err)
}
defer conn.Close()
```

```
client := pb.NewEchoServiceClient(conn)

response,  err  :=  client.Echo(context.Background(),
&pb.EchoRequest{Message: "Hello, gRPC!"})if err != nil {
log.Fatalf("could not call echo: %v", err)
}

log.Printf("Response from server: %s", response.Message)
}
```
```

### Performance Benefits of gRPC in Go

Using gRPC with Go improves performance significantly due to its lightweight nature and efficient serialization. Here are some specific benefits:

**Reduced Latency**: The combination of HTTP/2 multiplexing and Protocol Buffers serialization drastically reduces the overhead commonly seen in REST APIs based on text formats such as JSON or XML.

**Concurrency Support**: Go's goroutines enable handling multiple gRPC calls efficiently, allowing developers to build highly concurrent applications without the typical overhead associated with threads.

**Type Safety**: Protocol Buffers provide a strongly typed API, which can lead to safer and more maintainable code. Errors due to type mismatches can be caught at the compile time instead of runtime.

gRPC is a powerful framework that enhances the
```

capabilities of Go in building distributed systems. With features like bi-directional streaming, efficient serialization, and cross-language support, gRPC offers a robust solution for high-performance communication. In this chapter, we have explored the fundamentals ofgRPC, seen how to set up a basic service in Go, and highlighted its performance benefits.

Chapter 7: Data Management in Go Microservices

With their distributed nature, microservices enable teams to develop, deploy, and scale applications independently. However, one of the most challenging aspects of microservices architecture is data management. In this chapter, we will explore the principles, patterns, and best practices for managing data within Go microservices.

7.1 Understanding Data Management in Microservices

Data management in microservices involves the strategies and methodologies for storing, retrieving, and manipulating data across various components of an application. Unlike monolithic architectures, where a single database might serve all application components, microservices often require a more decentralized approach.

7.1.1 Challenges in Data Management

When deploying microservices, several challenges arise in the context of data management:

Data Isolation: Each microservice should manage its own data, which promotes decoupling but can lead to complexities when data needs to be shared among services.

Consistency: Maintaining data integrity and consistency across services poses challenges, particularly when dealing with eventual consistency.

117

Data Model Diversity: Different microservices may require different data storage technologies (SQL vs. NoSQL) and data models, leading to a heterogeneous data environment.

Distributed Transactions: Traditional transaction mechanisms do not fit well in a distributedenvironment, complicating operations that span multiple services.

7.2 Data Storage Patterns

Go microservices can employ various data storage patterns to address the challenges of data management. Understanding these patterns is crucial for selecting the right strategy for each microservice.

7.2.1 Database per Service

One common pattern is the **Database per Service** approach, where each microservice has its own dedicated database. This isolation enhances modularity and allows teams to choose the best database technology for each service's specific needs. However, it requires carefully designed APIs for services thatneed to communicate or share data.

7.2.2 Shared Database

In the **Shared Database** pattern, multiple microservices access a common database. While this approach simplifies data sharing and transaction management, it can lead to tight coupling among services, undermining the benefits of microservices architecture.

7.2.3 Event Sourcing

Event sourcing involves persisting the state of a system by capturing all changes as events. Microservices can utilize event stores to manage domain events, ensuring a reliable audit trail. This pattern supports eventual consistency and enables service inter-communication through event-driven architectures.

7.2.4 CQRS (Command Query Responsibility Segregation)

CQRS separates the concerns of data modification and data retrieval, allowing for different models for reading and writing data. This pattern can optimize performance, as microservices may handle commands and queries using different data stores or caching strategies.

7.3 Data Communication Strategies

Effective communication between microservices is vital for data management. Let's discuss the key strategies for inter-service communication.

7.3.1 Synchronous Communication

In synchronous communication, one service directly requests data from another. This can be achieved using REST APIs or gRPC. This approach is straightforward but can lead to performance bottlenecks and increased latency, especially if the requested service is down or slow to respond.

7.3.2 Asynchronous Communication

Asynchronous communication decouples services by allowing them to exchange messages without waiting for immediate responses. Technologies like Apache Kafka, RabbitMQ, or Azure Service Bus enable services to publish and subscribe to events, providing robustness and scalability. This is essential for building responsive and resilient systems.

7.4 Data Consistency Models

Consistency in microservices presents unique challenges. Depending on the business use case and requirements, different consistency models can be applied.

7.4.1 Strong Consistency

Strong consistency guarantees that a read operation returns the latest committed value. This model is often necessary for critical operations but can introduce significant latency and reduce availability.

7.4.2 Eventual Consistency

Eventual consistency allows system components to become consistent over time. This is a more flexible approach suitable for many distributed systems, enabling higher availability and responsiveness, but it requires careful handling of data states to avoid conflicts.

7.5 Best Practices for Data Management in Go

Microservices

To ensure smooth and efficient data management in Go microservices, consider the following best practices:

Encapsulate Data Logic: Each microservice should encapsulate its data access logic. This promotes reusability and helps avoid tight coupling.

Leverage Go's Concurrency: Use Go's goroutines and channels to handle concurrent data operations effectively, enhancing performance and responsiveness.

Implement Retry Logic: When dealing with external service calls or databases, implement a robust retry mechanism to handle transient errors gracefully.

Use API Gateways: An API gateway can centralize requests and responses, handling authentication, logging, and data transformation, which simplifies client interactions.

Monitor and Log Data Access: Implement monitoring and logging to track data access patterns, identify bottlenecks, and observe trends that may indicate problems.

By understanding the various approaches and best practices outlined in this chapter, developers can create robust, scalable, and maintainable microservices that effectively manage data. As we continue to explore the world of Go microservices, embracing the dynamism of data management will lead to successful, innovative software solutions that can stand the test of time.

Connecting to Databases with Go

One of Go's prominent features is its powerful standard library and support for connecting to various databases. Database interaction is a vital part of developing applications, and in this chapter, we will explore how to establish connections with different types of databases using Go.

Whether you are working with SQL (like MySQL, PostgreSQL, or SQLite) or NoSQL databases (such as MongoDB), Go provides robust libraries and frameworks that simplify these interactions.

Setting Up Your Environment

Before diving into database connectivity, ensure you have Go installed on your machine. You can download it from the official Go website. Once Go is installed, set up your workspace and ensure you have a database server running.

For SQL databases, you can use popular systems like:

MySQL
PostgreSQL
SQLite

For NoSQL databases, **MongoDB** is a widely used option.### Installing Database Drivers
To connect to a specific database, you will need the correct Go driver. Below are examples of how to install drivers for

the mentioned databases.

```bash
# MySQL
go get -u github.com/go-sql-driver/mysql

# PostgreSQL
go get -u github.com/lib/pq

# SQLite
go get -u modernc.org/sqlite

# MongoDB
go get go.mongodb.org/mongo-driver/mongo
```

Understanding Connection Strings

A connection string is essential for establishing a connection to your database. It usually contains information about the database type, username, password, host, port, and database name. Here are examples of connection strings for different databases:

MySQL:
`"username:password@tcp(localhost:3306)/dbname"`
PostgreSQL: `"host=localhost   port=5432
user=username password=password dbname=dbname
sslmode=disable"`

SQLite: `"file:dbname.db?cache=shared"`
MongoDB:
`"mongodb://username:password@localhost:27017/dbna

me"` ## Connecting to a SQL Database

Let's start by connecting to a MySQL database. The code below demonstrates how to establish a connection and perform basic operations such as querying and inserting data.

Example: MySQL Connection

```go
package main

import ( "database/sql""fmt"
"log"

_ "github.com/go-sql-driver/mysql"
)

func main() {
// Connection string
dsn                                                          :=
"username:password@tcp(localhost:3306)/dbname"

// Open the database
db, err := sql.Open("mysql", dsn)if err != nil {
log.Fatalf("Error opening database: %v", err)
}
defer db.Close()

// Test the connection
if err := db.Ping(); err != nil {
log.Fatalf("Error connecting to database: %v", err)
}
```

```go
fmt.Println("Successfully connected to the database!")

// Example query
rows, err := db.Query("SELECT id, name FROM users")if
err != nil {
log.Fatalf("Error performing query: %v", err)
}
defer rows.Close()

for rows.Next() {var id int
var name string
if err := rows.Scan(&id, &name); err != nil {
log.Fatalf("Error scanning row: %v", err)
}
fmt.Printf("User: %d, Name: %s\n", id, name)
}

// Insert Example
_, err = db.Exec("INSERT INTO users (name) VALUES
(?)", "John Doe")if err != nil {
log.Fatalf("Error inserting new user: %v", err)
}
fmt.Println("Inserted new user: John Doe")
}
```

Things to Note
Always handle errors when opening or querying the
database.
Use `defer` to ensure the database connection is closed
after operations are complete.
Use prepared statements whenever inserting data to avoid
SQL injection.## Connecting to NoSQL Databases

125

Next, let's look at how to connect to MongoDB. MongoDB uses a different model for data interaction, relying on collections instead of tables.

Example: MongoDB Connection

```go
package main

import ( "context""fmt"
"log"
"time"

"go.mongodb.org/mongo-driver/mongo"
"go.mongodb.org/mongo-driver/mongo/options"
)

func main() {
// Connection string
clientOptions                                    :=
options.Client().ApplyURI("mongodb://localhost:27017")

// Create MongoDB client
client,    err    :=    mongo.Connect(context.TODO(),
clientOptions)if err != nil {
log.Fatalf("Error connecting to MongoDB: %v", err)
}
defer client.Disconnect(context.TODO())

// Ping MongoDB
ctx, cancel := context.WithTimeout(context.Background(),
10*time.Second)defer cancel()
```

```go
err = client.Ping(ctx, nil)if err != nil {
log.Fatalf("Error pinging MongoDB: %v", err)
}

fmt.Println("Successfully connected and pinged MongoDB!")

// Example Inserting Document
collection := client.Database("testdb").Collection("users")
user := bson.D{{"name", "John Doe"}, {"age", 30}}
insertResult, err := collection.InsertOne(context.TODO(),
user)if err != nil {
log.Fatalf("Error inserting document: %v", err)
}
fmt.Printf("Inserted a single document: %v\n",
insertResult.InsertedID)

// Example Querying Documentvar result bson.D
err = collection.FindOne(context.TODO(),
bson.D{{"name", "John Doe"}}).Decode(&result)if err !=
nil {
log.Fatalf("Error finding document: %v", err)
}
fmt.Printf("Found document: %+v\n", result)
}
```

Important Points
Use `context` for managing requests and deadlines when
interacting with MongoDB.
Always defer disconnection from the database.
Handle errors thoroughly when performing operations.

127

In this chapter, we have covered the essential aspects of connecting to both SQL and NoSQL databases using Go. From setting up your environment to performing basic CRUD operations, these foundational concepts will help you effectively integrate database functionality into your Go applications.

Understanding how to connect and interact with databases is essential for any developer, and Go's simplicity and performance make it an excellent choice for building robust data-driven applications. As you continue to explore Go, consider delving deeper into ORM libraries such as GORM or SQLBoiler to streamline your database interactions further.

Handling Data Consistency and Transactions

This chapter will delve into the mechanisms provided by Go for handling data consistency and transactions, exploring how to effectively manage these aspects in your applications.

1. Understanding Data Consistency

At its core, data consistency refers to the accuracy and reliability of data stored in a database. Consistency ensures that any transaction brings the database from one valid state to another, maintaining predefined rules and constraints. In relational databases, this consistency is often enforced through schemas, foreign keys, and constraints.

1.1 ACID Principles

The ACID principles define the set of properties that guarantee that database transactions are processed reliably. They include:

Atomicity: Ensures that all operations within a transaction are fully completed or none at all. If a failure occurs, the transaction is rolled back to maintain the original state.

Consistency: Ensures that a transaction takes the database from one valid state to another, adhering to all rules and constraints.

Isolation: Allows transactions to operate independently without interference from other ongoing transactions.

Durability: Guarantees that once a transaction has been committed, it will remain so, even in the event of a system failure.

These principles guide how we design and manage transactions in Go.## 2. Transactions in Go
Go provides robust support for transactions primarily through the `database/sql` package. This package abstracts away the underlying database implementation, allowing developers to create, manage, and execute transactions across various database systems seamlessly.

2.1 Setting Up a Database Connection

Before we can work with transactions, we need to establish

a connection to our database. The following example demonstrates how to connect to a PostgreSQL database:

```go
package main

import ( "database/sql""log"
_ "github.com/lib/pq" // PostgreSQL driver
)

func main() {
connStr := "user=username password=yourpassword dbname=mydb sslmode=disable" db, err := sql.Open("postgres", connStr)
if err != nil { log.Fatal(err)
}
defer db.Close()
}
```

2.2 Initiating a Transaction

To work with transactions, we begin by initiating a transaction with the `Begin` method. This method returns a `*sql.Tx` object, which represents the transaction.

```go
tx, err := db.Begin()if err != nil {
log.Fatal(err)
}
```

2.3 Executing Transaction Operations

Once a transaction is initiated, we can execute multiple operations (insert, update, delete) within the transaction context. An example of performing a series of operations within a transaction is shown below:

```go
func UpdateBalance(db *sql.DB, accountID int, amount float64) error {tx, err := db.Begin()
if err != nil {return err
}

// Deferring rollback in case of an errordefer func() {
if err != nil { tx.Rollback()
}
}()

_, err = tx.Exec("UPDATE accounts SET balance = balance + $1 WHERE id = $2", amount, accountID)if err != nil {
return err
}

// Commit the transaction
if err := tx.Commit(); err != nil {return err
}

return nil
}
```

In this example, we define a function `UpdateBalance` that updates an account's balance. The transaction is committed only after the operations complete successfully. If an error occurs at any point, the transaction is rolled back.

2.4 Error Handling

Effective error handling is crucial in transaction management. If an error is encountered, it's essential to roll back the transaction to prevent any partial state changes. The `defer` statement illustrated in the previous example enables explicit handling of rollbacks in the context of the transaction.

2.5 Managing Concurrency

When multiple transactions vie for the same data, managing concurrency becomes essential. Go supports various isolation levels that determine how and when the changes made by one transaction become visible to others. The locks and isolation levels are often managed at the database level.

Using the `SetIsolationLevel` method, developers can specify the desired isolation level for each transaction:

```go
tx, err := db.BeginTx(context.Background(), &sql.TxOptions{Isolation: sql.LevelSerializable})
```

Different isolation levels have trade-offs in terms of performance and consistency. Familiarity with these levels helps developers make informed choices based on the specific needs of their applications.

2.6 Using Context for Timeouts and Cancellation

Go's `context` package provides a means to control the lifespan of transactions and should be utilized to handle timeouts or cancellations. Wrapping the transaction in a context can help enforce time limits, improving the robustness of your application:

```go
ctx, cancel := context.WithTimeout(context.Background(),
5*time.Second)defer cancel()

tx, err := db.BeginTx(ctx, nil)
```

Handling data consistency and transactions in Go is a fundamental aspect of building reliable applications. By leveraging Go's database/sql package, developers can implement robust transaction management that adheres to ACID principles, ensuring accuracy and reliability of the data. Understanding how to properly initiate transactions, manage concurrency, and handle errors is key to maintaining data integrity. Armed with these skills, you'll be well-equipped to build scalable and efficient Go applications that handle data with confidence.

Chapter 8: Securing Your Microservices

In this chapter, we will explore various strategies and best practices to secure your microservices built with Go, ensuring that they are robust against potential vulnerabilities and attacks.

Understanding Microservices Security Challenges ### The Microservice Paradigm

Microservices architecture breaks down applications into smaller, independent services that communicate over a network. This structure offers immense benefits in terms of flexibility, scalability, and maintainability. However, it also introduces new security challenges, including:

Increased Attack Surface: Each microservice may expose APIs, leading to a larger number of potential entry points for malicious actors.
Service-to-Service Communication: As microservices interact with one another, the risk of interception and unauthorized access increases.
Data Management: Sensitive data can be transmitted and stored across multiple services, raising issues related to data privacy and integrity.
Configuration Management: Deploying numerous microservices requires careful attention to configuration and consistency, as mistakes can lead to vulnerabilities.

Security Considerations

In securing your microservices, consider the following aspects:

Authentication: Verifying the identity of users or systems before granting access.
Authorization: Ensuring that authenticated users have permission to access the resources they request.
Encryption: Protecting data in transit and at rest through encryption mechanisms.
Logging and Monitoring: Keeping comprehensive logs and actively monitoring your microservices to detect abnormal behavior.
Rate Limiting: Preventing abuse and denial of service attacks by limiting the number of requests to your services.

Implementing Security in Go Microservices ### 1. Authentication and Authorization

When it comes to implementing authentication and authorization in your Go microservices, JWT (JSON Web Tokens) is a common and effective approach. Here's how to use JWT for securing your APIs:

Generate JWT Tokens: When a user successfully logs in, issue a JWT token that encodes user information and permissions.
Middleware for Verification: Implement middleware that checks the validity of the token on every incoming request.

```go
import (
"github.com/dgrijalva/jwt-go""net/http"
)

// Middleware to validate JWT tokens
func ValidateToken(next http.Handler) http.Handler {
return http.HandlerFunc(func(w http.ResponseWriter, r
```

```go
*http.Request)            {            tokenString            :=
r.Header.Get("Authorization")

// Code to parse and validate JWT
token, err := jwt.Parse(tokenString, func(token
*jwt.Token) (interface{}, error) {
// Ensure the token method is HMAC
if _, ok := token.Method.(*jwt.SigningMethodHMAC); !ok
{
return nil, fmt.Errorf("unexpected signing method: %v",
token.Header["alg"])
}
// Return the secret key
return []byte("your-secret-key"), nil
})

if err != nil || !token.Valid {
http.Error(w, "Unauthorized", http.StatusUnauthorized)
return
}

// Attach user information to context, if necessary
ctx      :=      context.WithValue(r.Context(),      "user",
token.Claims)r = r.WithContext(ctx)

next.ServeHTTP(w, r)
})
}
```
` ` `

2. Service-to-Service Communication

To enhance security during inter-service communication,
consider the following techniques:

Mutual TLS (mTLS): Implement mutual TLS to establish secure connections between microservices. This ensures that both the client and server authenticate each other, providing a strong layer of security.

API Gateway: Use an API Gateway to act as a single entry point for all your services. The gateway can handle authentication, logging, and request routing, reducing the complexity of securing individual services.

3. Data Protection

Protecting sensitive data is crucial in microservices architecture. Here are some strategies:

Encrypting Data: Use encryption for data at rest (in databases) and in transit (in APIs). The `crypto` package in Go provides easy-to-use algorithms for encrypting sensitive information.

```go
go import (
"crypto/aes"        "crypto/cipher"        "crypto/rand"
"encoding/hex""io"
)

func encrypt(plaintext string, key string) (string, error) {
block, err := aes.NewCipher([]byte(key))
if err != nil { return "", err
}

gcm, err := cipher.NewGCM(block)if err != nil {
return "", err
```

```
}

nonce := make([]byte, gcm.NonceSize())
if _, err := io.ReadFull(rand.Reader, nonce); err != nil {
return "", err
}

ciphertext := gcm.Seal(nonce, nonce, []byte(plaintext), nil)
return hex.EncodeToString(ciphertext), nil
}
```

Data Masking: Before storing sensitive data, consider using masking techniques to obfuscate it. This is particularly useful when dealing with personally identifiable information (PII).

4. Logging and Monitoring

Robust logging and monitoring are essential for detecting potential security breaches. Utilize structured logging libraries like `logrus` or `zap` to capture meaningful log entries:

Log Sensitive Actions: Log every authentication attempt, successful or failed, as well as significant actions that modify data.
Centralized Logging: Use centralized logging solutions such as ELK (Elasticsearch, Logstash, Kibana) or Splunk for real-time monitoring and alerting.

5. Rate Limiting

To mitigate the risk of Denial of Service (DoS) attacks,

implement rate limiting on your microservices. Go provides libraries such as `golang.org/x/time/rate` for easily adding ratelimiters to your APIs:

```go
go import (
"golang.org/x/time/rate""net/http"
)
var limiter = rate.NewLimiter(1, 3) // 1 request per second
with a burst of 3 func RateLimit(next http.Handler)
http.Handler {
return http.HandlerFunc(func(w http.ResponseWriter, r
*http.Request) {if !limiter.Allow() {
http.Error(w,        "Too        Many        Requests",
http.StatusTooManyRequests)return
}
next.ServeHTTP(w, r)
})

}
```

Securing your microservices is not just about implementing isolated solutions; it requires a comprehensive strategy that encompasses all layers of your application. By incorporating authentication and authorization, encrypting data, implementing mutual TLS, logging, and monitoring, and enforcing rate limiting, you can significantly reduce your microservices' vulnerability to threats.

In an ever-evolving threat landscape, security practices must continually adapt to new challenges. It is critical to stay informed about emerging security trends, regularly audit your codebase, and perform penetration testing to ensure your microservices remain safe and resilient against attacks.

Authentication and Authorization in Go

In the modern age of web applications, security is a paramount concern, especially when handling sensitive data or private information. With the rise in cyber threats, developers must ensure that only authenticated users can access resources and that their actions are authorized. This chapter delves into the fundamental concepts of authentication and authorization, particularly within the Go programming environment.

What Are Authentication and Authorization?

Before we dive into implementation in Go, it's essential to clearly define what authentication and authorization mean:

Authentication is the process of verifying the identity of a user or system. This step confirms who the user is.

Authorization refers to the permissions assigned to that user after they have been authenticated. This step determines what the user is allowed to do.

In simpler terms, authentication asks, "Who are you?" while authorization answers, "What can you do?" ## Authentication in Go
Authentication Mechanisms

There are various methods for implementing

authentication in Go applications:

Basic Authentication: This is a simple context where the user provides a username and password which the server validates. Basic authentication can be implemented easily but is not recommended for production due to security concerns.

Token-Based Authentication: This method often uses JSON Web Tokens (JWT), where the server generates a token upon successful login that the client can use for subsequent requests. Tokens allow for stateless authentication which is more scalable in distributed systems.

Session-Based Authentication: This method creates a session after the user logs in successfully. The session state is stored on the server and referenced by a session ID.

Implementing Basic Authentication

Let's examine how to implement basic authentication in Go.

```go
package main

import ( "fmt" "net/http""log"
)

func basicAuth(next http.Handler) http.Handler {
return http.HandlerFunc(func(w http.ResponseWriter, r
*http.Request) {username, password, ok := r.BasicAuth()
```

```go
if !ok || username != "user" || password != "pass" {
    w.Header().Set("WWW-Authenticate",          `Basic
realm="Authorization                         Required"`)
    w.WriteHeader(http.StatusUnauthorized)
    return
}
next.ServeHTTP(w, r)
})
}

func    protectedEndpoint(w    http.ResponseWriter,    r
*http.Request) { fmt.Fprintf(w,  "You've  accessed  a
protected endpoint!")
}

func main() {
http.Handle("/protected",
basicAuth(http.HandlerFunc(protectedEndpoint)))
log.Fatal(http.ListenAndServe(":8080", nil))
}
```

In this example, we define a `basicAuth` middleware that
checks the username and password against hardcoded
values. If the credentials are incorrect, a 401 Unauthorized
response is returned.

Token-Based Authentication Using JWT

Token-based authentication is widely adopted in modern
applications. Using JWT provides both security and
flexibility. The following outlines how to implement JWT
authentication in Go.

142

Dependencies

First, we need to install the `github.com/golang-jwt/jwt` package:

```sh
go get github.com/golang-jwt/jwt/v4
```

Implementation

Here's a simple example of JWT authentication:

```go
package main

import ( "fmt" "net/http"
"github.com/golang-jwt/jwt/v4""time"
)

var jwtKey = []byte("my_secret_key")

func    GenerateToken(w    http.ResponseWriter,    r
*http.Request) { expirationTime := time.Now().Add(5 *
time.Minute)
claims    :=    &jwt.Claims{    StandardClaims:
jwt.StandardClaims{
ExpiresAt: expirationTime.Unix(),
},
}

token := jwt.NewWithClaims(jwt.SigningMethodHS256,
claims)tokenString, err := token.SignedString(jwtKey)
```

```go
if err != nil {
http.Error(w, err.Error(), http.StatusInternalServerError)
return
}
http.SetCookie(w, &http.Cookie{Name: "token",
Value: tokenString, Expires: expirationTime,
})
fmt.Fprintf(w, "Token generated and set in cookie.")
}

func ValidateToken(next http.Handler) http.Handler {
return http.HandlerFunc(func(w http.ResponseWriter, r
*http.Request) {cookie, err := r.Cookie("token")
if err != nil {
http.Error(w,     "You     are     not     authenticated",
http.StatusUnauthorized)return
}

claims := &jwt.Claims{}
_, err = jwt.ParseWithClaims(cookie.Value, claims,
func(token *jwt.Token) error {return nil
})

if err != nil || claims.ExpiresAt < time.Now().Unix() {
http.Error(w, "Invalid token", http.StatusUnauthorized)
return
}

next.ServeHTTP(w, r)
})
}

func protectedEndpoint(w http.ResponseWriter, r
```

```go
*http.Request) { fmt.Fprintf(w, "You've accessed a protected endpoint!")
}

func main() {
http.HandleFunc("/generate-token", GenerateToken)
http.Handle("/protected",
ValidateToken(http.HandlerFunc(protectedEndpoint)))
http.ListenAndServe(":8080", nil)
}
```

```
```

Authorization in Go

Once a user has been authenticated, managing authorizations is crucial. In Go, it can be implemented in various ways, either through claims in a JWT or through a role-based access control system.

Role-Based Access Control (RBAC)

In this approach, each user is assigned a role defining what they can or cannot do. The following example demonstrates basic role assignment:

```go
func Authorize(role string, next http.Handler) http.Handler {
return http.HandlerFunc(func(w http.ResponseWriter, r *http.Request) {claims := &jwt.Claims{}
// Assume some method to extract claims from the token
// Validate token and roles based on JWT claims
```

```go
if role != "admin" {
    http.Error(w, "Forbidden", http.StatusForbidden)return
}

next.ServeHTTP(w, r)
})
}

func    adminEndpoint(w    http.ResponseWriter,    r
*http.Request) {fmt.Fprintf(w, "Welcome, Admin!")
}

func main() {
http.Handle("/admin",                 Authorize("admin",
http.HandlerFunc(adminEndpoint)))
http.ListenAndServe(":8080", nil)
}
```
```

In this case, the `Authorize` middleware checks the role and grants access only if the criteria are met. ## Best Practices
**Secure Your Tokens**: Always store your JWTs securely, preferably in HTTP-only cookies to prevent XSS attacks.

**Use HTTPS**: Ensure your application runs over HTTPS to encrypt data in transit.

**Implement Proper Logging**: Logs help trace unauthorized access attempts and user actions for audit purposes.
```

Regularly Update Dependencies: Outdated libraries can introduce vulnerabilities.

By understanding the principles and carefully applying best practices, developers can safeguard their applications against unauthorized access and protect sensitive data. As you explore these concepts, remember that security is an ongoing process, and staying informed of the latest developments is key to maintaining a robust security posture.

Protecting Microservices from Common Vulnerabilities

Go, also known as Golang, has emerged as a popular choice for building microservices due to its performance, simplicity, and strong concurrency support. However, with this widespread adoption comes the pressing need to address security vulnerabilities that can threaten the integrity, availability, and confidentiality of these services. In this chapter, we will explore common vulnerabilities in microservices developed with Go and discuss best practices for protecting them.

Understanding Microservices Architecture

Microservices architecture divides applications into smaller, loosely coupled services that communicate over a network. Each service is designed to perform a specific function and can be developed, deployed, and scaled independently. While this architecture provides numerous advantages, including agility and resilience, it also introduces new security challenges. The distributed nature of microservices means that vulnerabilities can propagate across the system, affecting multiple services at once.

Common Vulnerabilities in Go Microservices ### 1. Insecure APIs

Microservices often expose APIs for interaction with both other services and end-users. If these APIs are not properly secured, they can become entry points for malicious actors. Common API vulnerabilities include:

Insufficient Authentication and Authorization: Failing to implement robust authentication mechanisms can allow unauthorized users to access sensitive data or operations. It is vital to enforce strong authentication (e.g., OAuth, JWT) and to ensure that users only have access to resources they are authorized to access.

Exposure of Sensitive Data: APIs that do not encrypt data in transit (using HTTPS) or at rest can lead to sensitive information leakage. Sensitive data must be handled with strict care, using techniques such as encryption, tokenization, and secure storage.

2. Improper Input Validation

Input validation is critical to preventing injection attacks (e.g., SQL injection, command injection) and to ensuring that only properly formatted data is processed. In Go, developers may inadvertently overlook input validation, leading to vulnerabilities:

Validation Errors: Incorrectly validated input can lead to unexpected behavior or security flaws. Employ libraries that enforce strict validation, such as `go-playground/validator`, and implement custom validation logic as needed.

Insecure Deserialization: Data deserialization without appropriate validation can introduce securityrisks. Ensure that only trusted data sources are allowed, and validate the data before deserialization.

3. Lack of Rate Limiting and Throttling

Microservices are susceptible to Denial-of-Service (DoS) attacks, where attackers overwhelm a service with excessive requests. Implementing rate limiting and throttling can help mitigate these attacks:

Rate Limiting: Limit the number of requests a user can make to an API within a defined time period.Libraries like `go-redis/rate-limiter` and `go-chi/chi` can assist in implementing these strategies.

Circuit Breaker Pattern: Utilize the circuit breaker pattern to prevent cascading failures caused bydownstream service outages. Go provides libraries such as `afex/hystrix-go` for managing this pattern.

4. Dependency Management and Vulnerabilities

Go encourages the use of third-party libraries through its package management system, Go Modules. While this allows for rapid development, it also raises concerns about the security of these dependencies:

Outdated Libraries: Regularly audit and update dependencies to avoid known vulnerabilities. Tools such as `dependabot` and `go-audit` can help maintain an up-to-date dependency list while flagging vulnerabilities.

Supply Chain Risks: Be cautious about using unverified or unknown packages. Implement scanning tools and use private repositories to maintain control over third-party code.

Strategies for Securing Go Microservices
1. Secure Development Practices

Adopting a secure coding mindset throughout the development lifecycle is essential for protecting microservices:

Static Code Analysis: Utilize tools like `gosec` and `go-lint` to identify security issues in the codebase before deployment. These tools can reveal potential vulnerabilities and offer recommendations for mitigation.

Code Reviews: Implement regular code reviews with a focus on security. Peer reviews can catch vulnerabilities that automated tools may overlook.

2. Security in Configuration

Configuration management is critical for the security posture of microservices:

Environment Variables: Store sensitive data, such as database passwords and API keys, in environment variables instead of hardcoding them in the codebase. Use libraries like `godotenv` to manage these configurations easily.

Secret Management: Consider leveraging secret management solutions such as HashiCorp Vault or AWS Secrets Manager to handle sensitive information securely.

3. Monitoring and Logging

Active monitoring and logging are vital for identifying and responding to security incidents:

Audit Logs: Maintain audit logs for all API requests and sensitive operations. This helps in tracking suspicious activity and assists in forensic investigation.

Real-time Monitoring: Use monitoring tools like Prometheus and Grafana to keep track of service health and anomaly detection mechanisms. Setting alerts can help mitigate issues before they escalate.

4. Testing and Incident Response

Security testing should be integrated into the CI/CD pipeline:

Penetration Testing: Conduct regular penetration testing to identify and exploit vulnerabilities in a controlled environment. This process provides valuable insights into the security posture of the microservices.

Incident Response Plan: Develop and maintain an incident response plan to address breaches or security incidents quickly. Ensure the team is trained and regularly exercises the plan.

By implementing strong authentication and authorization mechanisms, ensuring proper input validation, managing dependencies carefully, and adopting secure development practices, organizations can significantly enhance the security of their microservices.

Chapter 9: Logging and Monitoring Microservices

This chapter will explore strategies for logging and monitoring Go microservices, including best practices, tools, and patterns to employ for a robust observability solution.

9.1 The Importance of Logging

Logging is a vital component of microservices development. Logs provide a historical record of operations and help in troubleshooting issues by offering context and insights into the application's behavior. Unlike traditional monolithic applications, where logging can be centralized, in microservices, each service potentially generates its own logs. Therefore, managing logs effectively across multiple services is crucial.

9.1.1 Types of Logs

Logs can be classified into several types, each serving a unique purpose:

Application Logs: These logs capture the application's internal operations, such as errors, warnings, and informational events.
Access Logs: Created by web servers or APIs, these logs record incoming requests, response times, and user activities.
Audit Logs: They provide a trail of user actions and system changes, which are crucial for security and

compliance.

9.2 Best Practices for Logging in Go

When it comes to logging in Go microservices, there are several best practices to ensure optimal logging structure and clarity.

9.2.1 Structured Logging

Structured logging is the practice of encoding log messages in a consistent and machine-readable format (e.g., JSON). This makes logs easier to parse and analyze.

```go
package main

import ("log"
"os"
)

func main() {
logger    :=    log.New(os.Stdout,    "INFO:    ",
log.Ldate|log.Ltime|log.Lshortfile) logger.Println("Service
started")
}
```

9.2.2 Log Levels

Implementing log levels (e.g., debug, info, warning, error, fatal) helps filter logs based on severity. This is particularly important in production environments, where it's essential to focus on significant events.

9.2.3 Contextual Logging

Using Go's context package (`context.Context`), it's beneficial to attach a context to your logs, propagating trace IDs or relevant metadata through service boundaries. This enables a clearer view of requests as they traverse through various microservices.

```go
package main

import ( "context""log"
)

func logWithContext(ctx context.Context, message string) {    traceID    :=    ctx.Value("trace_id").(string) log.Printf("[TRACE_ID: %s] %s", traceID, message)
}
```

9.3 Monitoring Microservices

Monitoring complements logging by providing real-time insights into system performance and health. It typically encompasses a variety of metrics and events that can inform service-level indicators (SLIs), service-level objectives (SLOs), and service-level agreements (SLAs).

9.3.1 Key Metrics

Here are some key metrics to monitor:

Request Rate: The number of requests the service handles over time.
Error Rate: The ratio of failed requests compared to the total requests.
Latency: Time taken to process requests; crucial for assessing performance.
Resource Utilization: Includes CPU, memory, and disk usage statistics.### 9.3.2 Instrumentation
Go supports several libraries for instrumentation that simplifies monitoring efforts:

Prometheus: An open-source monitoring system that can scrape metrics exposed by your services.
OpenTelemetry: A framework for observability that allows for distributed tracing and metricscollection.

Integrating Prometheus with a Go microservice might look like the following:

```go
package main

import ( "net/http"
"github.com/prometheus/client_golang/prometheus"
"github.com/prometheus/client_golang/prometheus/promhttp"
)

var (
requestCount    =    prometheus.NewCounterVec(
prometheus.CounterOpts{
Name: "http_requests_total",
```

```
Help: "Total number of HTTP requests.",
},
[]string{"method", "status"},
)
)

func init() { prometheus.MustRegister(requestCount)
}

func handler(w http.ResponseWriter, r *http.Request) {
requestCount.WithLabelValues(r.Method,    "200").Inc()
w.Write([]byte("Hello, World!"))
}

func main() { http.HandleFunc("/", handler)
http.Handle("/metrics",               promhttp.Handler())
http.ListenAndServe(":8080", nil)
}
```
` ` `

9.4 Centralized Logging Solutions

As the number of microservices grows, so does the
complexity of log management. Centralized logging
solutions aggregate logs from multiple services into one
platform for easier analysis and troubleshooting.

9.4.1 ELK Stack

The ELK Stack (Elasticsearch, Logstash, Kibana) is a
popular choice for centralized logging. Logstash collects
and processes logs, Elasticsearch stores them, and Kibana
provides a user-friendly GUI for searching through logs.

9.4.2 Fluentd and EFK Stack

An alternative is Fluentd, which works similarly to Logstash. When paired with Elasticsearch and Kibana,it's known as the EFK stack.

In microservices architecture, effective logging and monitoring are foundational to maintaining healthy and operable systems. By employing structured logging, leveraging Go's context for enriched logs, utilizing appropriate metrics, and implementing centralized logging solutions, developers can achieve a high degree of observability and reliability in their applications.

Integrating Logging with Go Applications

In Go, effective logging can significantly enhance your application's observability and maintainability. This chapter will cover best practices for integrating logging into your Go applications, explore popular logging libraries, and provide practical examples to illustrate the implementation of logging.

1. Understanding the Importance of Logging

Before diving into integration techniques, it's vital to understand why logging matters.

Debugging: Logs provide a historical trail of application behavior that can be invaluable for troubleshooting errors.
Auditing: In many applications, especially those that involve financial transactions or personal data, logging

actions can help maintain compliance and traceability.
Performance Monitoring: Logging can also be used to monitor application performance, helping to identify bottlenecks or long-running processes.
User Activity Tracking: Understanding how users interact with your application can inform design decisions and feature development.

2. Basic Logging in Go

The Go standard library provides a basic logging package called `log`. Here's how you can get started:

```go
package main

import ("log"
"os"
)

func main() {
// Create a log file
file, err := os.OpenFile("app.log",
os.O_CREATE|os.O_WRONLY|os.O_APPEND, 0666) if
err != nil {
log.Fatal(err)
}
defer file.Close()

// Set output of logs to filelog.SetOutput(file)

// Log messages log.Println("Application started")
log.Println("This is a simple log message")
```

159

```go
log.Println("Application finished")
}
```

In this example, logs are written to a file named `app.log`. It highlights the simplest form of logging, but for more complex applications, you may require more advanced logging features.

3. Advanced Logging Features

Advanced logging features can significantly improve the quality and usefulness of your logs. Here are several key features to consider:

3.1 Structured Logging

Structured logging involves logging information in a structured format, such as JSON, which makes it easier to parse and analyze logs. Libraries like `logrus` and `zap` support structured logging out of the box.

Example with logrus:
```go
package main

import (
log "github.com/sirupsen/logrus"
)

func main() { log.SetFormatter(&log.JSONFormatter{})
log.WithFields(log.Fields{
"event": "event_name","topic": "topic_name",
```

```
}).Info("This is a structured log message")
}
```

3.2 Log Levels

Log levels (e.g., Debug, Info, Warn, Error) allow you to
categorize your logs. This helps filter logs based on severity.

Example with zap:
```go
package main

import ( "go.uber.org/zap"
)

func main() {
logger, _ := zap.NewProduction()
defer logger.Sync() // flushes buffer, if any
logger.Info("This is an info message", zap.String("context",
"example"))
}
```

4. Choosing the Right Logging Library

While the standard `log` package is sufficient for basic
logging, the following libraries offer additional features:

logrus: A structured logger for Go that is easy to use
and integrates well with JSON. It supports loglevels and
custom formats.

zap: Developed by Uber, it is designed for speed and performance. Zap provides both a structuredlogger and a vanilla logger, catering to various logging needs.
zerolog: A lightweight logger that emphasizes performance and a minimalist API. It outputs logs in a structured format, making it an excellent choice for high-performance applications.

When choosing a logging library, consider the following factors:

Performance requirements
Support for structured logging
Ease of use and integration
Community support and documentation

5. Best Practices for Logging in Go Applications

To make the most of logging in your Go applications, follow these best practices: ### 5.1 Be Consistent
Ensure consistent log formatting across your application. This uniformity aids in log parsing and improves readability.

5.2 Log Context

Include relevant context in your log messages. This might include user IDs, request information, and other contextual data that can help identify the circumstances around each log entry.

5.3 Avoid Logging Sensitive Information

Be careful not to log sensitive data, such as passwords, credit card numbers, or personal identifyinginformation, to avoid security risks.

5.4 Use Log Levels Judiciously

Use appropriate log levels to categorize logs. Avoid excessive logging at the debug level in production environments to reduce noise and improve performance.

5.5 Use Log Rotation

For applications generating large quantities of logs, implement log rotation to manage log file sizes andensure that older log entries are archived or deleted as necessary.

By leveraging structured logging, adopting suitable logging libraries, and adhering to best practices, you can significantly improve your Go application's logging strategy. A robust logging implementation will not only help developers in troubleshooting but also provide invaluable insights into the application's operations over time.

Implementing Monitoring Tools for Health Checks

Ensuring that the applications are running smoothly and efficiently is crucial for maintaining high availability and excellent performance. In this chapter, we will delve into the various approaches and toolsfor implementing health checks in Go, focusing on how to monitor the status of applications effectively.

5.1 Understanding Health Checks

Health checks are automated processes that periodically verify the integrity and operational status of your applications. They are broadly categorized into two types:

Liveness Checks: These determine whether the application is running. If a liveness check fails, it indicates that the application is not functioning as expected, and it may need to be restarted.

Readiness Checks: These ensure that the application is ready to handle requests. A failing readiness check means that although the application is running, it is not in a state to process incoming traffic (e.g., due to ongoing initialization or maintenance).

To implement health checks effectively in Go, we begin by understanding how to leverage its concurrency and performance features.

5.2 Setting Up a Simple Health Check

We will create a simple HTTP server that includes endpoints for liveness and readiness checks. Below is a minimal example of how to implement these checks in Go:

```go
package main

import ( "net/http""log"
"time"
```

```go
)

var isReady = true // Simulate readiness status

func livenessCheck(w http.ResponseWriter, r *http.Request) {w.WriteHeader(http.StatusOK)
w.Write([]byte("OK"))
}

func readinessCheck(w http.ResponseWriter, r *http.Request) {if isReady {
w.WriteHeader(http.StatusOK)w.Write([]byte("READY"))
} else {
w.WriteHeader(http.StatusServiceUnavailable)
w.Write([]byte("NOT READY"))
}
}

func main() {
http.HandleFunc("/health/live", livenessCheck)
http.HandleFunc("/health/ready", readinessCheck)

// Simulate readiness change over timego func() {
time.Sleep(10 * time.Second) // Wait before becoming readyisReady = true// Mark as ready after some time
}()

log.Println("Starting server on :8080")
if err := http.ListenAndServe(":8080", nil); err != nil {
log.Fatalf("ListenAndServe: %v", err)
}
}
```
```
```

This simple application exposes two endpoints: `/health/live` for liveness and `/health/ready` for readiness. We also simulate a change in the readiness state after a certain time.

5.3 Integrating Monitoring Tools

While implementing health checks is essential, integrating them with monitoring tools greatly enhances observability. Popular tools that can be used alongside Go applications include Prometheus, Grafana, and ELK Stack (Elasticsearch, Logstash, and Kibana).

5.3.1 Using Prometheus

Prometheus is a powerful open-source monitoring system that can scrape metrics from your application and provide robust querying capabilities. To integrate Prometheus with the Go app, we can use the `prometheus/client_golang` package. First, install the package:
```bash
go                                                    get
github.com/prometheus/client_golang/prometheus
go                                                    get
github.com/prometheus/client_golang/prometheus/pro
mhttp
```

Next, extend our health check application to serve Prometheus metrics:

```go
import (
"github.com/prometheus/client_golang/prometheus"
"github.com/prometheus/client_golang/prometheus/promhttp"
)

var (
livenessGauge                          =
prometheus.NewGauge(prometheus.GaugeOpts{   Name:
"liveness",
Help: "Indicates if the application is live (1 = alive, 0 =
dead)",
})
readinessGauge                         =
prometheus.NewGauge(prometheus.GaugeOpts{   Name:
"readiness",

Help: "Indicates if the application is ready (1 = ready, 0 =
not ready)",
})
)

func init() {  prometheus.MustRegister(livenessGauge)
prometheus.MustRegister(readinessGauge)
}

func main() {
// Other code remains the same go func() {
for {
livenessGauge.Set(1) // Set liveness to 1 time.Sleep(5 *
time.Second)
}
}()
```

```go
// Update readiness based on the isReady variablego func()
{
for {
if isReady { readinessGauge.Set(1)
} else {
readinessGauge.Set(0)



}
}()

time.Sleep(5 * time.Second)


http.Handle("/metrics",                promhttp.Handler())
log.Println("Exposing metrics on /metrics endpoint")

log.Fatal(http.ListenAndServe(":8080", nil))
}
```

In this updated code, the `/metrics` endpoint is added, where Prometheus can scrape the metrics. The liveness and readiness states are reflected in Prometheus gauges.

5.4 Visualizing Metrics with Grafana

Once Prometheus is set up and scraping metrics from your Go application, you can visualize these metrics using Grafana. Grafana allows you to create dashboards that provide insights into application performance and health.

Install Grafana: Follow the official Grafana installation guide for your operating system.

Connect to Prometheus: Once Grafana is up and running, create a new data source and select Prometheus. Provide the Prometheus URL (by default, it runs on `http://localhost:9090`).

Create Dashboards: Use the `liveness` and `readiness` metrics to create visual representations of your application's health in real time.

5.5 Advanced Health Checks

While the previous implementation provides a basic understanding of health checks, more advanced scenarios may require sophisticated health check mechanisms. These could include:

Dependency Checks: Ensuring that dependent services (e.g., databases, external APIs) are available and responsive.
Load Testing: Implementing checks that evaluate the application's performance under load.
Custom Metrics: Developing application-specific metrics that will help in understanding the usage patterns, performance bottlenecks, and more.

In this chapter, we explored the implementation of health checks in Go and integrated monitoring solutions such as Prometheus. Monitoring tools are essential for maintaining observability into the state and performance of applications. By setting up simple health checks and

169

hooking them into robust monitoring frameworks, developers can ensure that their applications remain operational and performant.

Chapter 10: Testing and Debugging Go Microservices

In this chapter, we will explore best practices for testing Go microservices, the various methodologies applicable, and effective techniques for debugging.

10.1 Importance of Testing in Microservices

Microservices are typically independent services deployed across multiple environments and platforms. This decentralization offers flexibility and resilience but also complicates testing. Effective testing ensures that each microservice operates as intended and integrates effectively with other services. It provides confidence that changes can be deployed without causing regressions or introducing new bugs.

Key Objectives of Testing Microservices:
Isolation: Each service must be tested independently.
Integration: Services must also be tested concerning their interactions.
Performance: Assessing the performance under varying loads.
Resilience: Ensuring services can recover from failures.## 10.2 Types of Testing for Go Microservices
When it comes to testing Go microservices, several types of tests are essential. Each serves a different purpose and contributes to a comprehensive testing strategy.

10.2.1 Unit Testing

Unit tests are the foundation of any testing strategy. They validate the smallest parts of an application (functions, methods, or components) in isolation. In Go, unit tests are easy to create and run, thanks to the built-in testing package.

```go
package myservice

import (
"testing"
)

func TestAdd(t *testing.T) {result := Add(2, 3) expected :=
5
if result != expected {
t.Errorf("Expected %d, got %d", expected, result)
}
}
```

10.2.2 Integration Testing

Integration tests ensure that multiple components work together as intended. In microservices, this involves testing interactions among services, databases, and external APIs.

```go
func TestServiceIntegration(t *testing.T) {
// Setup test database and services
// Simulate requests between services
// Assert on responses and side effects
}
```

10.2.3 End-to-End Testing

End-to-end (E2E) testing simulates real user scenarios. It verifies that the entire application flow works as expected, from the user interface to the database. Tools like Cypress or Selenium can be integrated with Go services to support E2E tests.

10.2.4 Load Testing

Load testing helps gauge how the service performs under high loads. This is particularly important for microservices that might scale differently. Tools like Apache JMeter or Go's own `vegeta` can be used for this purpose.

```bash
echo "GET http://service-url" | vegeta attack -duration=30s -rate=10/s | vegeta report
```

10.3 Testing Best Practices

While the types of tests are crucial, the following best practices further enhance testing effectiveness:

173

Automate Tests: Use continuous integration/continuous deployment (CI/CD) pipelines to run testsautomatically on commits and pull requests.
Mock External Dependencies: Use interfaces and mocks to isolate service logic from externaldependencies, making tests faster and more reliable.
Use Test Containers: Employ Docker to spin up isolated environments for testing, ensuring consistency across development and testing stages.
Version Tests with Code: Keep test cases version-controlled alongside your codebase, ensuring they reflect the state of the code.
Write Clear and Concise Tests: Focus on readability. Each test should clearly state its intent.## 10.4 Debugging Go Microservices
Despite thorough testing, bugs may still occur. When they do, effective debugging is essential to identify andresolve issues quickly.

10.4.1 Logging

Good logging practices are foundational for debugging. Use structured logging to track the flow of data and important events within services. The use of log levels (info, warn, error) can aid in filtering logs and makingsense of what's happening.

```go
import (
"log"
)

func ProcessRequest(req Request) {
log.Println("Processing request:", req.ID)
```

```go
// ...
log.Println("Request processed successfully")
}
```

10.4.2 Panic Handling

In Go, panics can occur due to unexpected states or errors. Utilize `defer` and `recover` to gracefully handle panics and log error information as needed.

```go
func SafeProcessRequest(req Request) {defer func() {
if r := recover(); r != nil { log.Println("Recovered from panic:", r)




}
```

```
}
}()
ProcessRequest(req)
```

10.4.3 Profiling

Profiling is crucial for understanding performance bottlenecks. The Go runtime includes built-in profiling tools that can help identify CPU and memory usage issues. One can use the `pprof` package to visualize performance data.

175

```go
import (
"net/http"
_ "net/http/pprof"
)

go func() {
log.Println(http.ListenAndServe("localhost:6060", nil))
}()
```

10.4.4 Distributed Tracing

In a microservices environment, tracking requests across services can be challenging. Distributed tracing tools like Jaeger or OpenTelemetry allow you to visualize the flow and identify where bottlenecks or failures occur.

By embracing different types of testing, adhering to best practices, and utilizing robust debugging techniques, developers can ensure high-quality, resilient microservices that stand up to real-world demands. As microservices continue to evolve, so too will the strategies and tools for testing and debugging them. The key is to remain adaptable and vigilant, leveraging the rich ecosystem around Go while fostering a culture of quality in your development organization.

Writing Unit and Integration Tests in Go

In Go, testing is built into the language and provides a robust framework for both unit and integration tests. This chapter will guide you through the process of writing unit tests and integration tests in Go, offering best practices and examples to solidify your understanding.

Understanding Unit Tests### What is a Unit Test?

A unit test is a type of software test that focuses on a single "unit" of code, typically a function or a method. The purpose of a unit test is to validate that each piece performs correctly and meets its specifications. Unit tests are usually written alongside the functionality they test and are executed frequently during development.

Writing Unit Tests in Go

Go provides a built-in testing package, which makes writing and running unit tests straightforward. Here's a step-by-step guide to writing unit tests in Go.

Step 1: Setting Up Your Test File

Unit tests are typically placed in a file with a `_test.go` suffix. For example, if you have a file named `math.go` that contains functions for mathematical operations, you would create a new file called `math_test.go`.

Step 2: Importing the Testing Package

At the top of your `math_test.go`, you need to import the `testing` package:

```go
package math

import (
```

```
"testing"
)
```

Step 3: Writing Test Functions

Test functions must start with the word `Test` and take a
pointer to `testing.T` as an argument. Here's how you
might write a simple test for an `Add` function that sums
two integers:

```go
// math.go package math

func Add(a, b int) int {return a + b
}

// math_test.gopackage math

import (
"testing"
)

func TestAdd(t *testing.T) {result := Add(1, 2) expected :=
3

if result != expected {
t.Errorf("Add(1, 2) = %d; want %d", result, expected)
}
}
```

Step 4: Running Your Tests

To run your unit tests, navigate to the directory containing your Go files and execute:

```sh
go test
```

This command will automatically discover any test functions in your `_test.go` files and run them. ## Understanding Integration Tests
What is an Integration Test?

Integration tests are designed to validate the interactions between different units or components of your application. While unit tests focus on individual functions, integration tests check if various parts of the system work together as intended. They might involve multiple components, databases, network requests, or external services.

Writing Integration Tests in Go

Writing integration tests follows a similar approach as unit tests but often involves more setup, such as initializing states, databases, or mocking external systems.

Example of Integration Tests

Suppose you have a simple web service that performs user registration. Your integration tests would ensure that the entire user registration flow operates correctly from the HTTP request to the database interaction.

Step 1: Setup Testing Environment

179

You might have a replica of your database or use a mocked database for testing. For example, here is a snippet for starting an HTTP server for testing:

```go
// user.go package user

import (
"net/http"
)

func RegisterHandler(w http.ResponseWriter, r *http.Request) {
// Mock registration logic w.WriteHeader(http.StatusOK)
}

// user_test.gopackage user

import (
"net/http" "net/http/httptest""testing"
)

func TestRegisterHandler(t *testing.T) {
req := httptest.NewRequest(http.MethodPost, "/register", nil)w := httptest.NewRecorder()

RegisterHandler(w, req)res := w.Result()
if res.StatusCode != http.StatusOK {
t.Errorf("Expected status 200 OK; got %v", res.Status)
}
}
```

Best Practices for Testing in Go

Keep Your Tests Near Your Code: Place tests in the same package and close to the code they test. This organization makes it easier to correlate tests and functionality.

Use Table-Driven Tests: For functions with multiple input scenarios, using table-driven tests can help avoid repetitive code:

```go
func TestAddTableDriven(t *testing.T) {tests := []struct {
a, b    int expected int
}{
{1, 2, 3},
{2, 3, 5},
{-1, 1, 0},
}

for _, test := range tests { result := Add(test.a, test.b)if
result != test.expected {




}
}
```

t.Errorf("Add(%d, %d) = %d; want %d", test.a, test.b,
result, test.expected)
}

Isolate Tests: When writing integration tests, ensure that tests do not depend on external systems'state. It is vital to run tests in isolation to prevent flaky tests.

Run Tests Regularly: Integrate testing into your development workflow. Running tests after each change helps catch errors early.

Use Mocks and Stubs: For external dependencies, consider using mocking libraries to simulate responses from services without requiring them to be live.

By following the principles and examples outlined in this chapter, you will be well equipped to implement arobust testing strategy for your Go applications, facilitating cleaner, more maintainable code. Remember, testing is not just a safety net; it is an essential tool for building high-quality software.

Debugging Strategies for Microservices

The beauty of microservices lies in their modularity, allowing teams to develop, deploy, and manage services independently. Nonetheless, with this modular approach comes the challenge of debugging applications that can spread across numerous services, often operating asynchronously. In this chapter, wewill explore effective debugging strategies for microservices built using the Go programming language, providing practical techniques and best practices to identify and resolve issues efficiently.

Understanding Microservices Architecture

Before diving into debugging strategies, it is essential to grasp the fundamental concepts of microservices architecture. In a microservices system, an application is composed of multiple loosely-coupled services, each responsible for specific business functionality. While this design enhances scalability and maintainability, it complicates debugging due to the distributed nature of the architecture.

Each service is independently executable, interacts with other services over the network, and usually persists its data in a separate database. The inter-service communication often involves protocols such as HTTP/REST, gRPC, or message queues, introducing additional layers of complexity in identifying bottlenecks or failures.

The Challenge of Debugging

Debugging microservices retains some common challenges, including:

Distributed Nature: Errors might manifest in one service but originate from another. Tracing the flow of requests and responses across services can be tedious.
Asynchronous Communication: In systems utilizing message-driven patterns, debugging can become challenging when using events or asynchronous messages.
Complex Dependencies: Services often depend on one another, introducing cascading failures.
Environment Variability: Differences between development, testing, staging, and production

environments can lead to inconsistencies in behavior.

Given these challenges, various strategies can significantly simplify the task of debugging in a Go microservices ecosystem.

Strategies for Debugging Go Microservices ### 1. Extensive Logging

Logging plays a crucial role in debugging microservices. Begin by implementing structured logging across your services using libraries such as `logrus` or Go's built-in `log` package. Structured logging helps in generating logs in a consistent format (like JSON), making it easier to query and analyze log data.

Contextual Information: Include request IDs, timestamps, service names, and error messages to provide contextual information.
Log Levels: Use log levels (debug, info, warning, error) to control the verbosity of logs.
Centralized Logging: Use centralized logging solutions (like ELK Stack or Loki) to aggregate logs from multiple services, enabling you to search and analyze logs effectively across the system.

2. Tracing Requests

To better understand how requests flow through your microservices, consider implementing distributed tracing. Distributed tracing tools like Jaeger or OpenTelemetry allow you to visualize the journey of a request through various services, helping you identify performance bottlenecks and trace errors.

Instrumenting Code: Wrap your service calls with tracing instrumentation to generate trace identifiers. This will allow you to follow requests across service boundaries.
Analyzing Performance: Use the tracing information to analyze latency issues and understand where bottlenecks or failures lie in your microservices.

3. Error Handling and Recovery

Proper error handling is essential for developing robust microservices. Ensure that services return meaningful error messages and valid HTTP status codes. Leverage Go's error handling capabilities by adhering to conventions in returning and wrapping errors.

Graceful Degradation: Implement patterns like circuit breakers or timeouts (using libraries such as `go-resiliency`) to enhance resilience in case a service becomes unresponsive.
Health Checks: Implement liveness and readiness probes in your services to ensure they are functioning correctly and able to serve requests.

4. Testing

Implement comprehensive testing practices at all levels in your microservices. Unit tests, integration tests, and end-to-end tests should be part of your development process.

Local Testing: Utilize tools like `Docker Compose` to recreate service dependencies locally.
Mocking Services: Use mocking libraries (e.g.,

185

`gomock` or `testify`) to simulate interactions with external services.
Chaos Engineering: Introduce failure scenarios using chaos engineering tools (like Gremlin or ChaosMonkey) to evaluate how services respond to unexpected failures.

5. Debugging Tools

Go offers a variety of tools to assist in debugging. Familiarize yourself with the following:

Go's Built-in Debugger: Utilize the `delve` debugger to step through your code, inspect variables, and analyze the call stack.
Profiling: Use the Go pprof package to analyze the performance of your application and identify memory leaks or CPU bottlenecks. Profiling can be performed both in local and production environments.

6. Runtime Observability

Enhance observability in your microservices by integrating metrics and monitoring into your applications. Popular libraries like `prometheus/client_golang` allow you to expose metrics such as request counts, error rates, and latency times.

Dashboards: Implement monitoring dashboards using tools like Grafana to visualize application metrics.
Alerts: Set up alerting mechanisms to notify developers of critical issues before they affect users.

Debugging microservices in Go requires a systematic

approach, combined with an understanding of the unique challenges posed by distributed architectures. By employing extensive logging, distributed tracing, robust error handling, comprehensive testing, and leveraging Go's debugging tools, developers can effectively identify and resolve issues within their microservices architecture.

Conclusion

As we reach the end of our journey through "Go Programming for Microservices: Build Scalable, High-Performance Applications with Ease," we hope you feel empowered and inspired to take your knowledge of Go and microservices to the next level. The principles and techniques discussed throughout this ebook have equipped you with the tools necessary to develop robust, scalable applications that can thrive in today's fast-paced digital landscape.

Go is not just a programming language; it's a philosophy that emphasizes simplicity, efficiency, and performance. By harnessing these qualities, you can create microservices that not only meet the demands of your users but also adapt seamlessly to changing requirements. The patterns and practices we've explored—from designing RESTful APIs to implementing gRPC for high-performance communication—are fundamental building blocks for any modern application.

As you embark on your own projects, remember that the best practices outlined in this ebook are merely starting points. The tech landscape is ever-evolving; staying up-to-date with the latest developments in Go and microservices architecture will be crucial to your success. Engage with the Go community, contribute to open-source projects, and continuously refine your skills.

In conclusion, the journey of building scalable and high-performance applications is not just about mastering a language or a toolset; it's about embracing a mindset that prioritizes resilience, adaptability, and collaboration. As you apply what you've learned here, we encourage you to experiment, iterate, and innovate. The world of microservices holds immense potential, and your contributions can help shape its future.

Thank you for joining us on this journey. May your developments in Go be fruitful and your applications impact the world in meaningful ways. Happy coding!

Biography

Tommy Clark is a passionate and dynamic author who combines a deep love for technology with an insatiable curiosity for innovation. As the mastermind behind the book *"Clark: A Journey Through Expertise and Innovation,"* Tommy brings years of hands-on experience in web development, web applications, and system administration to the forefront, offering readers a unique and insightful perspective.

With a strong background in Go programming and an ever-evolving fascination with crafting robust, efficient systems, Tommy excels at turning complex technical concepts into practical, actionable strategies. Whether building cutting-edge web solutions or diving into the intricate details of system optimization, Tommy's expertise is both broad and profound.

When not immersed in coding or writing, Tommy enjoys exploring the latest tech trends, tinkering with open-source projects, and mentoring aspiring developers. His enthusiasm for technology and dedication to empowering others shine through in everything he creates.

Join Tommy Clark on this exciting journey to unlock the full potential of technology—and get ready to be inspired, informed, and equipped to tackle your next big challenge!

Glossary: Go Programming for Microservices

A

API (Application Programming Interface): A set of rules and protocols for building and interacting with software applications. In the context of microservices, APIs are often used for communication between different services.

Async/Await: A programming pattern that allows you to write asynchronous code in a more synchronous style. While Go does not have async/await like JavaScript, it provides goroutines for concurrent execution.

B

Build Tool: A tool used to automate the process of compiling and building applications. In Go, the built-in `go build` command compiles the code into a binary executable.

C

Concurrency: The ability of a system to handle multiple tasks simultaneously. Go is designed with concurrency in mind, using goroutines and channels to manage concurrent operations.

Containerization: A method of packaging software in a way that allows it to run consistently across different computing environments. Docker is a popular containerization tool often used in conjunction with Go microservices.

D

Dependency Injection: A design pattern that allows a program to follow the Inversion of Control principle, making it more modular and easier to test. In Go, dependency injection can be achieved using interfaces and constructor functions.

Docker: An open-source platform that automates the deployment of applications in lightweight, portable containers.

E

Error Handling: A critical aspect of Go programming, where functions return error values to indicate success or failure. Go encourages explicit error checking instead of using exceptions.

F

Framework: A collection of libraries and tools that provide a foundation for building applications. Go has several web frameworks, such as Gin and Echo, to facilitate microservices development.

G

Goroutine: A lightweight thread managed by the Go runtime. Goroutines enable concurrent programming and are a key feature of Go.

Go Module: A dependency management system that allows you to specify and manage dependencies for your Go projects. Modules are defined in a `go.mod` file.

H

HTTP: The Hypertext Transfer Protocol is the foundation of data communication on the web. In Go, the `net/http` package provides the necessary tools to build HTTP servers and clients.

I

Interface: A type that specifies a contract by defining method signatures without implementing them. Interfaces promote flexibility and enable the implementation of different types in a unified manner.

J

JSON (JavaScript Object Notation): A lightweight data interchange format that is easy for humans to read and write and easy for machines to parse and generate. Go provides built-in support for JSON encoding and decoding through the `encoding/json` package.

K

Kubernetes: An open-source container orchestration platform that automates the deployment, scaling, and management of containerized applications. It is commonly used to manage Go microservices in production environments.

L

Logging: The process of recording application events and errors. Go offers several logging libraries, including the standard `log` package and more advanced options like Logrus or Zap.

M

Middleware: Functions that wrap around HTTP handlers to provide additional functionality, such as logging, authentication, or error handling.

Microservices: An architectural style that structures an application as a collection of small, independent services that communicate over a network. Each microservice is responsible for a specific business capability.

N

Namespace: A container that holds a set of identifiers and allows disambiguation of homonym identifiers in different parts of a program.

O

ORM (Object-Relational Mapping): A programming technique used to convert data between incompatible type systems in object-oriented programming languages. In Go, several libraries, such asGORM, provide ORM capabilities.

P

Protocol Buffers: A language-agnostic binary serialization format developed by Google that is used to serialize structured data. It is often used in microservices to define service contracts.

Q

Query Language: A language designed to retrieve and manipulate data stored in databases. Popular query languages include SQL and NoSQL query languages.

R

REST (Representational State Transfer): An architectural style that relies on stateless communication, often using HTTP. RESTful APIs are commonly used in microservices.

S

Service Discovery: The process of automatically detecting devices and services on a network. In microservices, service discovery allows an application to locate the right instances of services.

Swagger: An open-source framework for API documentation that describes the structure of APIs in a machine-readable format. It helps developers understand how to interact with services.

T

Testing: The process of executing a program with the intent of finding errors. Go has built-in support for testing through the `testing` package, allowing developers to write unit tests and benchmarks easily.

U

Unit Testing: A software testing method that entails testing individual units of code in isolation to verify their correctness.

V

Version Control: A system that records file changes over time, enabling multiple developers to collaborate on a project. Git is the most widely used version control system in Go projects.

W

WebSocket: A protocol for full-duplex communication channels over a single TCP connection, commonly used for real-time web applications. Go provides support for WebSockets in the `golang.org/x/net/websocket` package. ### X
XML (eXtensible Markup Language): A markup language that defines rules for encoding documents in a format that is both human-readable and machine-readable. Go includes a package for XML handling (`encoding/xml`).

Y

YAML (YAML Ain't Markup Language): A human-readable data serialization standard that is commonly used for configuration files. Go supports YAML through third-party libraries like `go-yaml`.

Z

Zero Value: The default value of a variable when it is declared but not initialized in Go. Each type in Go has a distinct zero value.

www.ingramcontent.com/pod-product-compliance
Lightning Source LLC
La Vergne TN
LVHW022343060326
832902LV00022B/4221